Contemporary Indian Women Novelists in English

New Perspectives

Edited by
Amar Nath Prasad
Ashish Gupta

ATLANTIC
PUBLISHERS & DISTRIBUTORS (P) LTD

Published by

ATLANTIC

PUBLISHERS & DISTRIBUTORS (P) LTD

7/22, Ansari Road, Darya Ganj, New Delhi-110002
Phones : +91-11-40775252, 40775214, 23273880, 23275880
Fax : +91-11-23285873
Web : www.atlanticbooks.com
E-mail : orders@atlanticbooks.com

Branch Office: Chennai
Phones : +91-44-48531784, 28291383
E-mail : chennai@atlanticbooks.com

Reprint 2021

Printed & bound in India by Atlantic Print Services

Preface

The present book, *Contemporary Indian Women Novelists in English: New Perspectives*, is an anthology of critical research articles contributed by teachers and research scholars of English literature. It attempts to elucidate and explore critically some of the contemporary women novelists in English. It includes papers on well-known writers, like Anita Desai, Mahasweta Devi, Shashi Deshpande, Arundhati Roy, Bharati Mukherjee, Jhumpa Lahiri, Shobhaa De, Manju Kapur, Jai Nimbkar, Meena Alexander, Bama, and Volga. These novelists have tried their best to present their viewpoints very realistically and sensitively. Their creative world includes not simply the realistic portrayal of the day-to-day feelings, aspirations with hurdles of life, but is also suffused with some beautiful images and symbols which captivate the attention of the connoisseurs of art and literature. Some of them have got several awards and accolades and have set milestones in the field of literature. The book is a tribute to all these women writers who fought for the cause of emancipation of women, their constant search for individuality, and their tireless efforts to break the long-established rules of patriarchal domination.

The book has seen the light of the day after unforgettable co-operation and valuable suggestions of a number of people to whom we want to record our thanks. They are Prof. Shibu Simon, Dr. R. Soundararajan, Dr. J. Sumuel Kirubahar, Prof. S. Kanakaraj, and Dr. Sandip P. Chavan.

Last but not least, our thanks are also due to the publisher, Atlantic Publishers and Distributors (P) Ltd., New Delhi for bringing out this book so nicely and promptly.

Amar Nath Prasad
Ashish Gupta

Contents

Contributors

Uddhav Jane, Principal, Arts and Science College, Kamargaon, Distt. Washim, Maharashtra.

Pushpa Lakhdive, Former Head of English Department, SNUK College, Akola, Maharashtra.

K. Radha, Associate Professor, Department of English, Perriyar EVR (Govt.) College, Tiruchirapalli, Tamil Nadu.

R. Rajalaksmi, Research Scholar, Department of English, Perriyar EVR (Govt.) College, Tiruchirapalli, Tamil Nadu.

Sandip P. Chavan, Asst. Professor and Head, Department of English, Shahid Bhagat Singh Mahavidyalaya, Killari, Latur, Maharashtra.

Amar Nath Prasad, Associate Professor and Head, P.G. Department of English, Jagdam College, Chhapra, Bihar.

J. Samuel Kirubahar, Associate Professor of English, Research Centre in English, VHNSN College (Autonomous), Virudhunagar, Tamil Nadu.

S. Kanakaraj, Professor and Head in English (Retd.), DDE, Madurai Kamaraj University, Madurai, Tamil Nadu.

M. Natarajan, Assistant Professor, Department of English, Constituent College, Bharathidasan University, Tiruchirappali, Tamil Nadu.

R. Soundararajan, Associate Professor, P.G. and Research Department of English, National College (Autonomous), Trichy, Tamil Nadu.

P. Murugesan, Research Scholar, P.G. and Research Department of English, National College (Autonomous), Trichy, Tamil Nadu.

S. Chitra, Research Scholar, P.G. and Research Department of English, National College (Autonomous), Trichy, Tamil Nadu.

Ashish Gupta, Associate Professor (English), Department of Postgraduate Studies and Research, J.H. Govt. P.G. College, Betul, Madhya Pradesh.

N. Velmani, Associate Professor of English and Dean of Arts, V.V. Vanniaperumal College for Women, Virudhunagar, Tamil Nadu.

C. Shanmuga Priya, Assistant Professor, Department of English, Srimad Andaran Arts and Science College, Trichy, Tamil Nadu.

Shibu Simon, Professor and Head, Faculty of English, National Defence Academy (NDA), Pune, Maharashtra.

V. Sunitha, Assistant Professor (Senior), English Department, School of Social Sciences and Languages, VIT University, Vellore, Tamil Nadu.

1

Women Sensibility in the Novels of Anita Desai

Uddhav Jane

Introduction

If one examines the five novels—*Cry, The Peacock*, *Voices in the City*, *Where Shall We Go This Summer?*, *Fire on the Mountain* and *Clear Light of Day*, one realizes that a major portion of Anita Desai's writing in these, focuses on the woman. Through the female characters, issues relating to women in a distinctly Indian situation and context are explored. These include the position of the single and married woman in India, motherhood and housekeeping. There are also those issues connected with the physical side of a woman's life. Since aspects of Indian womanhood are central to the novels, a study of them from this angle seems relevant. Further, when reading the novels, the Indian woman may frequently experience a sense of familiarity. This is because they give expression to ideas and sentiments that she may have often experienced, but never clarified, even for herself. For the Indian woman, therefore, an enquiry into this facet of Anita Desai's writing can prove a process of self-discovery. Much of the interest and relevance of the present study for me, arose out of this fact.

My viewpoint in this paper is that there is a very definite concern in Anita Desai's novels with the situation and circumstances of the Indian woman. While there is nothing blatantly militant about her writing, it is clear from the manner in which she sets forth a situation, that she wishes the reader to look at it critically, to question and evaluate. The bonds which confine the Indian woman on the social, intellectual, and physical planes are exposed. However, at present, the aim of this study, implicitly, is the issue of emancipation—the need for it and how far from it the Indian woman often is. The scope and purpose of this research work consist of establishing these facts, by examining in turn the facets of Indian womanhood reflected in the novels. Since the basic issues are all-pervading, a head-wise division based on a novel by novel analysis would have proved repetitious. Instead, the main body of this work has been spaced out, with subheadings to indicate shifts in theme or argument.

Anita Desai is the representative novelist of the second generation of the Indian novel. The reflection of the thematic shift broadly from national, historical to the more subjective and personal is discernible in her novels. All her novels deal with the life of woman in Indian society. She probes the inner life of the woman, her psychological and emotional fluctuations. In her novels, we find the application of female phase of the Indian feministic concern. She has viewed the Indian woman as a separate entity and has shared her experiences as a woman would or must experience with the creation of vibrant sensibility of woman characters. In his reflective, critical assessment of her novels, K.S. Iyengar, sounds very pertinent when he points out:

> Her forte, in other words, is the exploration of sensibility. The particular kind of modern Indian sensibility that is ill at ease among the barbarians and the philistines, the anarchists and the immoralists. Since her preoccupation is with the inner world of sensibility rather than the outer world of action, she has tried to forge a style supple and suggestive enough to convey the fever and fretfulness of the stream of consciousness of her principal characters. The intolerable grapple with thoughts, feelings and emotions is necessarily reflected in the language, syntax and imagery, yet the reader's first impression on reading Anita Desai's novels may very well be that the emotions are too many and are often the result of excessive celebration on the author's part and not always determined by the movements in the consciousness of the characters. Nevertheless, Anita

> Desai's is an original talent that has the courage to go on its own way. (Iyengar, K.R.S., 464-65)

Anita Desai's portrayal of the Indian woman is not onesided. She concentrates on both the inner life and the outer life of her characters. The projection of the woman in the novels of Anita Desai certainly evinces the onset of a new age in Indian writing. She depicts women characters not superficially but as made of flesh and blood with its respective strength and weaknesses, by portraying characters who are governed by a sense of compromise, sacrifice and surrender, rather than complete revolt against the system for the sake of physical and emotional liberty. It is found that Anita Desai, in her novels, has tried seriously to explore and demystify the realities of life for which she delved deep into the complexities of life. She states: "writing to me is a process of discovering the truth...the truth that is nine-tenth of the iceberg that lies submerged beneath the one-tenth visible portion we call reality. Writing is my way of plunging to the depths and exploring this underlying truth. All my writing is an effort to discover, to underline and convey the true significance of things" (James Vinson, 348). Many critics of the Indian breed have striking by noted that Anita Desai's novels are female-oriented. She probes into their problems, be it of a mother, a daughter, a sister or a wife. She writes of the woman as a victim in a patriarchal, patrilineal and father-dominated Indian family. The Indian woman is, forever, dominated by and dependent upon a male member of her family—be it the father, the brother, the husband, or the son. These are the various phases of an Indian woman's life and the novelist sharply focuses upon the emotional reactions of the woman as she experiences these stages. It is not always an attitude of compromise, there are moments of rebellion and sometimes she gathers sufficient courage to speak out a word of resistance. Anita Desai has a limited range but still she finds ample opportunities to observe minute details while portraying life in its totality. Shantha Krishnaswamy has rightly pointed out that:

> Anita Desai's novels constitute together the documentation, through fiction, of radical female resistance against a patriarchal defined concept of normality. She finds the links between female duality, myth and psychosis

> intriguing; each heroine is seen as searching for, finding and absorbing or annihilating the double who represents the socially impermissible aspects of her feminity. (Shantha Krishnaswamy, 237)

Anita Desai depicts the Indian woman as a fighter, a victim, a heroine and ultimately a winner because of her indomitable spirit and attitude of compromise. She has portrayed both kinds of women—those who are symbols of growth and change; and those who are powerful means of withdrawal, regression, decay, death and destruction. A woman is a giver of life, a means of moving forward and perpetuating the human race, at the same time the cruel onslaughts of fate lead to her despondency and withdrawal. Anita Desai designs the exploration of the disturbed psyche of the Indian woman laying emphasis on the factors of loneliness and alienation. Women are suddenly confronted with the enigma of survival. However, the women in her novels do not give up the strife so easily. They indulge in self-analysis, self-discovery and ultimately compromise with the situation to live life stoically becoming assets to the family by developing the power of sustenance. True enough, some women characters prefer to remain in the world of illusion while many others endeavor to find a way out.

Before we deal with her novels, it is eventually apt to have a glance at her biographical part in brief so that one could get a full grasp of the representation of women's sensibility. Anita Desai was born in Mussoorie, a hill station north of Delhi, as the daughter of D.N. Muzumdar, a Bengali businessman and the mother Toni Nime, of German origin. Her cross-cultural marriage provided her with the ample opportunity of experiencing the plight of woman in Indian context. She began to write in English at the age of seven, and published her first story at the age of nine. Desai was educated in Delhi at Queen Mary's Higher Secondary School and Miranda House, Delhi University, where she received a B.A. degree in English literature in 1957. In the following year, she married Ashvin Desai, a businessman; they had four children.

As a novelist, Desai made her debut in 1963 with *Cry, The Peacock*. She had started to write short stories regularly before her marriage. *The Peacock* was published in Britain by Peter Owen, a publisher specializing in literature of the British Commonwealth and Continental Europe. It was followed by *Voices in the City* (1965), a story about three siblings, Amla, Nirode, and Monisha and their different ways of life in Calcutta. Amla sees the city as a monster, Nirode sacrifices everything for her career and Monisha cannot bear her stifling existence in the household of a wealthy-old Calcutta family. *Fire on the Mountain* (1977), set in Kasuli, a hill station, focused on three women and their complex experiences in life. No one, said Bim, slowly and precisely, comprehends better than children do. No one feels the atmosphere more keenly—or catches the nuances, all the insinuations in the air—or notes those details that escape elders because their senses have atrophied or calcified.

In *Clear Light of Day* (1980), Desai wove the history of Delhi with a middle-class Hindu family. The central character is Bim (short for Bimla) Das, a history professor, an independent woman. Bim's memories of the family past dominate her sterile existence, she feels betrayed by her unambitious sister Tara and replays her memories in the decaying family mansion in Old Delhi. Their mentally-retarded brother-in-law plays old records. Tara do not understand why Bim doesn't want anything to change, when she rejects the hopeless atmosphere of the house. It seemed to her that the dullness and the boredom of her childhood, her youth, were stored here in the room under the worn dusty red rugs, in the bloated brassware, amongst the dried grasses in the swollen vases, behind the yellowed photographs in the oval frames—everything, everything that she had so hated as a child and that was still preserved here as if this were the storeroom of some dull, uninviting provincial museum. The summer of 1947 has divided the nation and the family—Hindus and Muslims are torn apart by Partition.

Through Tara's and Bim's consciousness, Desai examines the same events from different points of views. The author's characters in many novels are members of the Anglicized Indian bourgeoisie, whose marital problems are in the forefront. Her characters often adopt escapist ways to cope with the boring everyday life or world outside comfortable living. In *Where Shall*

We Go This Summer? (1975), Sita, pregnant with her fifth child, takes refuge from her marriage on the magical island homestead of her deceased father. Nanda Kaul in *Fire on the Mountain* withdraws into a private world of self-willed isolation. Desai has commented on her work: "My novels are no reflection of Indian society, politics or character. They are my private attempt to seize upon the raw material of life." In *The Zigzag Way* (2004), Desai departed from her familiar territories and set the story of identity and self-discovery in Mexico. In the mid-1980s, Desai started to look more closely the life of the unprivileged.

The Woman in Relation to Husband

In the Indian context, the woman who remains single is considered a socially-incomplete being. Men have a perfect right to prefer solitude, but the Indian woman is not a free being in this respect. The woman who remains single, whether by choice or account of circumstances, is often assumed to be a frustrated or unfulfilled creature. In *Clear Light of Day,* Anita Desai projects this typical reaction, when Dr. Biswas says to Bim with a deep sigh,

> Now I understand why you do not wish to marry. You have dedicated your life to others—to your sick brother and your aged aunt and your little brother.... You have sacrificed your own life for them. We are further told, that Bim's month falls open in astonishment at being "so misunderstood, so totally misread". (*CL* 97)

Regarded as an abnormal creature, the single woman's eccentricities are more readily pounced upon. Tara covertly watches Bim talking to herself and takes note of her excessive meanness in scraping leftovers from meals into tiny saucers. She sees these as significant and—even if she doesn't say so directly—as somehow related to Bim's spinsterhood.

Bim at one point, while petting her cat, shows that she is aware of this kind of attitude: "You are thinking how old spinsters go ga-ga over their pets because they haven't children.... You think animals take the place of babies for us love-starved spinsters" (*CL* 6-7). Someone like Ila Das in *Fire on the Mountain*, with her ancient court shoes, wobbly top-knot, ragged petticoat and moth-eaten shoulder bag, would be readily labeled a "typical dried up spinster". The tourists think of her as "the crazy woman" (*FM* 197). As she hobbles along, people invariably knock into her, shove her aside, burst into guffaws and make jeering remarks. Even critics tend to view her in this light of the "typical spinster-like the other spinsters of Carignano, Ila Das has her own whims and idiosyncrasies". Now all had left Ila Das,...she had become a dry, shriveled, shrieking old woman (Sunwani, V.K. 87-88). Ila Das's qualifications are of the genteel sort that are not put on paper and rubber-stamped. Her background has not equipped her to manage alone in a world of harsh realities. Anita Desai shows how the single woman in India who lacks financial security becomes a victim of the social system.

Mira-masi in *Clear Light of Day*, is not technically a single woman. However, being widowed at a virginal fifteen, her plight is similar to that of the woman who is alone and without a husband in India. It seems logical, therefore, to deal with her here. Mira-masi's situation, wherein she is made to suffer for her solitariness, is a fairly typical one. She experiences a loss of status simultaneously with the loss of her husband. Her horoscope is blamed for her husband's death by his family and she is made to pay for her guilt by scrubbing, washing, and cooking until she ages young, growing greyer, shabbier, seedier. It is ironically stated that her unattractive appearance at least saves her from sexual assault by her brother-in-law. The very mention of this fact, however, is a reminder of such exploitation of widowed women in India. The magazine *Social Welfare* bears an article by Lop Amudra bringing out this point. Mira-masi's brothers-in-law make her the butt of their ridicule. Finally, when they tire of her they turn her out. She's nothing more than a "cracked-pot, torn rag, picked bone" (*CL* 108). Lop Amudra's article shows how Indian widows merit only an inferior status and are expected to practice lives of renunciation (Lop Amudra 15).

This is portrayed by Anita Desai in the case of Mira-masi. When the children wonder why she always wears white, their mother explains, smoothing down her own rich silks, that white is the widow's colour. Mira-masi herself admits that she has given away her wedding finery to her sisters-in-law to augment their dowries. The one sari she has been allowed to retain because it is white, has a stripe of crimson and gold. This makes it "impossible for her to wear: taboo" (*CL* 108). Anita Desai uses Mira-masi to depict how an Indian woman is victimized, exploited and humiliated on account of being alone—a woman minus a husband. What makes such victimization possible? Primarily, the economic factor. Most widows are far from being self-dependent and are therefore considered a burden both by parents and in-laws. Mira-masi, for instance, is turned out by her in-laws when they suspect her of being a parasite. It is the lack of financial independence which makes such women victims of their solitary status. In Bim, Anita Desai depicts an aspects of Indian womanhood which has been emerging in recent years. She is the kind of new Indian woman who has begun to think anew about traditionally-accepted norms regarding a woman's life and behavior (Sharma, R.S. 138).

Even at a very young age she questions, for instance, why marriage should be the only vocation for a woman, the only means of expressing herself. When Tara asks what else there can be, she replies, "Can't you think? I can think of hundreds of things to do instead" (*CL* 140). She wonders why the Mishra girls are in such a hurry to get married instead of going to college. "... they're not educated yet," she exclaims. Bim refuses to accept the common Indian notion that education and career are not serious pursuits for women, and, if undertaken, are more in the nature of stop-gap arrangements. Her attitude to the course of study she undertakes and later to her career, is one of commitment. She does not use them as compensations for marriage. She is one of those genuine existents with a profound and permanent interest in their work and projects (Parshley, H.M. 11). It is partly because she has a firm belief in herself and her work, that she can function as an independent existent, associating with men on a level of equality. Simone de Beauvoir makes the point that society requires the "true woman" as it calls her, to make herself object, to be the Other (Simone de Beauvoir, 291).

This is something Bim refuses to do. She refuses to play the conventional role of a sex object and a submissive woman. Sitting in the Mishra garden, watching Bim talk to the men,

Tara has to admit that Bim certainly cannot be said to flirt. As Bim slaps hard at a mosquito in an "unladylike" fashion, telling Manu not to bother with the flit gun, Tara reflects that this is characteristic of Bim—she never bothers to consciously present herself in an attractive light to the opposite sex. Bim is someone who will never belie her own intelligence and blind herself to the shortcomings of someone like Dr. Biswas, or even someone like Baku! and marry in order to escape from a situation or even from a fear of remaining single. What enables Bim to live as a single woman in India, while still retaining qualities of a genuine existent (which is something Mira-masi and Ila Das cannot manage to do), is again largely the economic factor. She works and earns enough to support herself as she reflects at one point, a fact which would boost any woman's self-confidence.

> It is through gainful employment that woman has traversed most of the distance that separated her from the male; and nothing else can guarantee her liberty in practice...when she is productive, active, she regains her transcendences; in her projects she concretely affirms her status as subject. (Simone de Beauvoir, 689)

Through the representations of single women, the reader is made conscious of how far social attitudes fetter such women. The attempt of someone like Bim to break through to broader perspectives, is also taken in. However, one must take into account the fact that while Bim does represent in many ways the new Indian woman, such a woman is still part of a very small minority and more likely, perhaps to be found among the upper classes. A positive feature in Anita Desai is that she never depicts a situation or character as merely black or white. Anita Desai herself says that she hopes through her writing to make "some significant statement on life—not necessarily a watertight, hard and fast set of rules but preferably an ambiguous, elastic, shifting and kinetic one..." (James Vinson, 348).

While Bim stays single and remains at home by choice, there are hints of the tinge of regret she experiences as she recalls her dreams of wider vistas. At the beginning of the book, she speaks of the desirability of "going away—into the world—something wider, freer, brighter" (*CL* 4). Anita Desai also shows how the

Indian social set-up exerts an influence on Bim's choice. Bim has always been the only one to take up various responsibilities. If she had been a Western woman, for instance, she may perhaps have put her aunt and brother into suitable Homes and then moved out to make her own life. While Bim doesn't "sacrifice" her life for her brother and aunt in the sense Dr. Biswas understands it, that is, by reluctantly renouncing marriage, the "caring" element does come in. The closeness of family ties do count with her, a fact which her Western counterpart may be less affected by. This is what makes for Bim's Indianness and what rounds out Anita Desai's portrayal of Indian womanhood.

Maya is one of the most talked-about characters of Anita Desai, whose deeper sensitivity towards life get expressed in her relationship with her husband. In contrast to her husband who is materialistic, practical, pragmatic, and unresponsive, Maya is an extremely sensitive, imaginative, passionate, and sensuous woman. The relationship between the husband and wife seems to be a mechanical fusion which lacked harmony of thought and action. It is difficult to agree with the critics who consider Maya to be a neurotic. She is perfectly normal and healthy woman. Her only sin is perhaps she is sensitive, imaginative, passionate, and sensuous. These are in fact the characteristics of normal female with reasonably good social status and upbringing. Maya in her view is driven to emotional instability and even murder under the pressures of marital disharmony. This is the point of mark in the following statement regarding the marriage:

> ...it was broken repeatedly, and repeatedly the pieces were picked up and put together again, as of sacred iron with which out of the prettiest superstition, we could not bear to part. (*CP* 40)

It is clear that the husband and wife are poles apart. There is complete lack of communication between the two. The detached relationship is conspicuous in the changed attitude of her husband after the death of Toto. To Gautama, her husband, it is "all over" and she simply needed a "cup of tea". He fails to realize her misery and does not know how to comfort her. Insensitivity of the husband becomes clear from female agony emerged in the physical and emotional starvation of Maya who says: "... he knew nothing that concerned me. Giving me an opal ring to wear on my finger, he did not notice the translucent skin beneath, the blue flashing veins that ran under and out of the bridge of gold and jolted me" (*CP* 9). The cold and unresponsive attitude of her husband becomes clearer when he asks Maya to go to sleep, while he has been engrossed with his work on papers. This underlying of the spousal relationship led Maya to emotional as well as physical depression. She says:

> ...he did not give another thought to me, to either soft willing body or the lonely waiting mind that waited near the bed....

Maya's love of life and nature is found in her sensuous description of nature. She is highly sensitive towards the object of nature. She gives sensuous account of flowers and fruits, forms, and colors. Sights and sounds in nature attract her like a passion. She is infuriated when she finds her husband fails to notice the dust storm. This indicates his insensitiveness to life. Eventually, she doesn't fail to find him as a representative of the patriarchal materialistic civilization and culture. Undoubtedly, her obsessive love of life and desire led her to kill her husband. The act of murder is none other than the revolt against the callous materialistic social order. Maya believes that she is unfit to live in this social order fully intact with the male interest, dominance, and control over the female world.

She doesn't like the civilization based on logic and normality. She wants to be free from the chains of slavery based on customs and established norms of the society. Her revolt against the social order is an aesthetic revolt—the revolt of sensibility against the logic of the so-called normality that seeks to colonize desire through a network of institutional mechanisms: "All order is gone out of my life, all formality, there is no plan, no peace nothing to keep me with the pattern of familiar, everything living and doing..." (*CP* 195). Maya represents the disturbed psyche of modern Indian woman. She tries to strike a balance between instinctual needs and intellectual aspirations. Deeply exhausted by this crucial act, she is further bewildered when the existential absurdity of life is brought before her. When she experiences loneliness and lack of communication, she finds herself in mental crisis. Feminine studies shows that Indian woman passive or aggressive, traditional or modern—serves to reflect the writer's sense of isolation, fear, bewilderment and emotional vulnerability. She evokes continuous discussion of social values. She is the focal point of contact between the writer's consciousness and the alien world, her experience of reality and hope for salvation. As a symbol not only of growth, life, and fertility, but of withdrawal, regression, decay, and death, she is powerful figure indeed as a protester against social and sexual inequalities and discrimination.

Desai's *Where Shall We Go This Summer?* describes the tension between a sensitive wife Sita and the rational husband Raman. It emphasizes the triumph of life over chaos and of art over life. The protagonist Sita's main problem is maladjustment with her husband, Raman who ignores her desires and misunderstanding between them, he is fed up her husband, his business, surroundings and also his friends. Raman's lack of love and feeling brings her to the verge of insanity. P.F. Patil in his article titled "The Theme of Marital Disharmony in the Novels of Anita Desai" comments that the novel provides "a passionate commentary upon the maladjustment that spiritually renders Raman and Sita totally homeless. Disaster inclines from the very beginning" (Dhawan, 136). Sita's search for self ends in wholeness of life. For Atma Ram the novel "seeks to unravel the inner mystery of life, to discover the energy that nourishes the spirit, and discards pettiness, horror and hypocrisy of everyday life" (Halpirin, 133). The title, *Where Shall We Go This Summer?* is highly sensitive. The interrogative feature of the title is symbolic of the uncertain state of the heroine's mind, of her awareness and of her indeterminate fate. Obviously, Sita re-establishes her contacts with the soil and gets over her loneliness by learning to laugh. It is the story of the boredom and loneliness experiences of a sensitive, over-emotional middle-aged married protagonist, Sita who is aliened from her husband and children and refuses to give birth to her fifth child in a world of destruction. She escapes to the island where she realizes the life in spite of its nastiness, brutishness, madness, tedium, and boredom should be lived. The island forms the core of Sita's conscious existence. The protagonist, Sita is sick of everything, everybody, her husband, her children, their film way of fight, Menaka's cutting of flower buds, insensibly and tearing of Sunday water colors, Karan's senseless joy, at the dismantling of the tower of clocks by throwing his body over it, and the servants talk in the kitchen, all disturb her mind. She expresses her resentment through smoking, abusing her children for trifles, losing her temper at the servants talk. None of these leaves any impact on her husband. Another incident which accentuates her sense of alienation is the street fight of the *ayahs*. Sita's own servant maid, Rosie fights with two other ladies in the street. She is irritating to hear those words and she rushes to the street where she drags her *ayah* out of the knot. At the same time, she places Karan at a safe distance. Sensitive Sita feels distress to narrate the whole incident to her husband. But Raman takes it as another instance of her drama and ask her to stop the story. Besides, there are many incidents which intensify her sense of alienation and search for identity. Prasanna Sree emphatically comments that Desai "penetrates psychologically deep into the inner working of women and externalizes their passive reaction" (Sree, 22). Sita can no longer endure the violence around her. So, she decides to search a place for her peaceful life, Sita tries to escape from her duties and also dismay of her husband Raman. It seems an absurdity of the plan that a pregnant woman is leaving for an unreal place. She expects her new vision of life in the remote island and her dream of island is unbound: "She had escaped from duties and responsibilities, from order and routine, from life and the city, to the unlivable island."

Like Maya in *Cry, The Peacock*, Sita is also unable to put up with her in-laws. Desai deals with the entry of Sita into the island after living a "life was a crust of dull tedium, of hopeless disappointment" (*WSGS* 52). In fact, Sita's journey to the island is a quest for integration of the self. Actually, island is a heaven to Sita which wonderfully holds the master key to her final liberation from the existential anxiety, hopelessness and suffering. She believes that her problems being magically solved by the island and she relieves from her mental anxiety and will be calm and comfortable in the island. The psychological cosmos of Sita's life mingles with her father's fantasy. Before her marriage, she led a glorious lifestyle in an island. She remains the lovely company of her sister Rekha, Jeevan, and her father who had always been surrounded by his disciples. Sita comes to the island with foolish hope. She already has four children. At the age of forty, she conceives the fifth one. But she would not like to deliver her child in the destructive land. So, she comes to Manori in order not to give birth to the fifth one, "she had come on a pilgrimage, to beg for the miracle of keeping her baby unborn" (*WSS* 31). Sita has been presented as a shattered and frustrated woman who feels trapped in the monotony of her house. Her neurotic fears and anxieties make her terrible. She feels dullness and boredom and deadness in the people whom she meets and they pose the greatest threat to her existence. As a result, Sita cannot even treat her husband's friends, guests, colleagues, business associates, and visitors with tolerance and understanding. They appear to her, "nothing but appetite...animals" (*WSS* 32). Perhaps, Raman stands for the conformity, sanity and prose of life whereas Sita is all sensitivity, feverish imagination, and vague romanticism.

Marriage in Light of Mutilation

Another aspect of Indian womanhood reflected in the novels is that connected with the married woman. Marriage is traditionally offered as the ultimate destiny for a woman by Indian society. Boys and young men generally confront open futures, while girls often find their futures imposed upon them. *Voices in the City*, for instance, begins with Monisha's and Amla's brother Arun leaving for London, where he is to attend college. Maya's brother Arjuna in *Cry, The Peacock*, Sita's brother Jivan in *Where Shall We Go This Summer?*, and Tara's and Bim's brother Raja in *Clear Light of Day*, all move out of claustrophobic home situations to make their own lives. The girls, on the other hand, do not have any other vistas besides marriage opening up before them.

In *Clear Light of Day,* the mother of the Mishra sisters, who was herself married at twelve, wishes her daughters to get married as early as possible. We are told they stay at home after finishing school, to help with the housekeeping and await marriages to be arranged for them. The sense of her "vocation" is impressed upon a girl and in time she too believes in it and is convinced of her limited capacities in other directions. Many Indian women work very superficially at their studies, because they feel they are to be married anyway. In *Clear Light of Day*, the Mishra sisters sometimes take their books across to Tara's room, but their interest in academic work being weak and wavering, they soon abandon them to go shopping or attend a family festivity. Bim, watching the preparations for the Mishra sisters' engagement party, wonders how they are going to study and pass their finals amidst such commotion. Tara replies that she doesn't think it matters to them as they are getting married afterwards, anyway. The Indian woman, therefore, tends to enter into marriage because it is the socially-acceptable thing to do. Celibacy may reduce her to the rank of a parasite and pariah as in the case of Mira-masi and Ila Das.

Marriage is often her only means of financial support and of integration into the community. Many women mistakenly view marriage as an escape. Having led very restricted lives, segregated from the opposite sex, they expect it to increase their freedom, recognizing its enslaving qualities only too late. Tara in *Clear Light of Day* had always found her home atmosphere stifling. She admits to Bim that in retrospect she realizes, she had used marriage to Bakul as an escape.

In *Where Shall We Go This Summer?*, Sita allows her life to be managed by someone else, and in this way, drifts into marriage. Not having understood the need to plan in advance, she is left destitute at the time of her father's death. It is Deedar's son who shuts up the house, takes her away, sends her to college and installs her in a hostel. Finally, out of pity, lust, a sudden will for adventure and because it is inevitable, he marries her. In India, women who live in a male-dominated society, are generally given in marriage by certain males to other males. The woman's freedom of choice is limited. The arrangements may be made between the two sets of parents, or between father-in-law and son-in-law. In *Voices in the City*, Aunt Lila who is deputed to meet Jiban and his family before Monisha's parents do, reports that he is unsuitable to Monisha's tastes and inclinations. Significantly, Monisha's parents decide on this basis that he is the right man.

Monisha, they feel, should not be encouraged in her "morbid inclinations". To marry into a stolid, unimaginative family, just sufficiently educated to accept her with tolerance, will be good for her.

What is apparent in a large number of cases, is the passivity of Indian women with regard to marriage. Like the Mishra sisters, they await marriages to be arranged for them and are given in marriage. Anita Desai, therefore, at various points, touches on the manner in which most Indian women enter into marriage. When marriage is more or less tyrannically imposed, when it is used as an escape, when it is entered into without any real conviction, an element of unauthenticity colors the marital relationship right at the start. A good deal of Anita Desai's depiction of marriages focuses on elements of discord. Between Gautama and Maya of *Cry, The Peacock,* there is an almost total incompatibility. Maya's father had proposed that she marry Gautama, a suggestion she eagerly accepted. However, there is an unbridgeable communication gap between them and she scarcely understands him, a man far older than she is. This last is again a feature common to many Indian marriages. In *Voices in the City*, Amla watching Jiban and Monisha together reflects on what an ill-suited pair they are. She wonders why Monisha has been married to "this boring nonentity, this blind moralist... this rotund, minute-minded and limited official" (*VC* 198).

In *Clear Light of Day,* the Mishra sisters are sent home by their husbands and the Mishra brothers' wives also leave them, on account of incompatibility. What comes across through Anita Desai's portrayal of such instances, is the almost primitive quality of the Indian system of arranged marriages. In them, a woman is yoked in marriage to a man she may have met momentarily, under parental supervision and whose tastes and inclinations she has scarcely explored.

Besides incompatibility, another aspect which emerges in the novels is the inequality of the woman's position *vis-à-vis* the man's, within marriage. The world still remains largely male-oriented and the Indian context more so. Tara Ali Baig writing in *The Times of India Sunday Review* points out, that while early India was mother-goddess oriented, with the coming of Aryans homage to the male began to predominate both in art and life. She shows how even today advertising reflects the dominance of the man. A man may be shown fast asleep in bed, for instance, while his wife hovers over him lovingly with a cup of tea. In the novels, the attitude of the men towards their wives often approximates that of superior beings towards lesser creatures. This is apparent in *Cry, The Peacock*, in Gautama's attitude to Maya. The critic Srinivasa Iyengar says that in his own way Gautama is "indulgent enough and affectionate enough" (Iyengar, K.R.S., 66). But what precisely is the quality of this affection, this indulgence. If often has the element of condescension in it. True, in many ways, Maya is silly and childish, but this doesn't altogether excuse Gautama's distinctly superior attitude. No is said to see "no value in anything less than the ideas and theories born of human, preferably, male brains" (*CP* 99). At one point, he tells Maya: "You go chattering like a monkey.... But, being a creature of pure instinct, you do, every now and then, stumble-purely by accident, I'm sure upon the salient point of the problem..." (*CP* 16). In the past, he is even supposed to have referred to her "third-rate poetess's mind" (*CP* 113). Critics point out that it is Gautama who has taught Maya the value of reflection. "In her moments of lucidity Maya acknowledges that Gautama is an ally and that it is in her love for him that she had experienced pain and reflection and that he had enlarged her world (Jasbir Jain, 25).

However, the passage in which Maya acknowledges this, contains ironic elements. Gautama teaches her to reflect, yes, but what is the result of such reflection? Her heart like a wild beast on a leash, strains in fury till tiredness sets in and in the dark she can ultimately say, "He is right and I was wrong" (*CP* 201). The inferior light in which many Indian women are regarded by their husbands, is apparent in other instances too. In *Voices in the City*, Monisha is suspected of being a thief by her in-laws, because she uses the money her husband has left in their wardrobe. Even Jiban, instead of accepting her right to the money, questions it. He does not say, "Why did you not tell them at once?" but, "Why didn't you tell me before you took it?" (*VC* 138). Bakul in *Clear Light of Day* is quite a mediocre person. Yet, he impresses upon Tara the fact that it is he who has made something of her: "So, I only have to bring you home for a day, Tara, and you go back to being the hopeless person you were before I married you (*CL* 17). He seeks to mould her into the kind of woman he would like her to be, rather than acknowledging that she is an individual in her own right. Tara even becomes his mouthpiece. Simone de Beauvoir points out that when "the husband succeeds in making his wife an echo of himself...after some months or years they have nothing left to say to one another...they are statically united, they are 'one', instead of maintaining a dynamic and living relation" (Simone de, 489-90) In the novels, the husband's manner of talking down to their wives, their attempts at molding them in their own images are indicative of the inferior status of the married woman in India.

What are the other aspects seen in the novels of the situation of the Indian married woman? Traditional marriage does not invite woman to transcend herself with man, but confines her in immanence, shuts her up within the circle of herself. Her horizon shrinks to the house. The immanence and indwelling often characteristic of the lot of the married woman in India is seen in the case of Sita in *Where Shall We Go This Summer?*. Sita finds that her life has been largely confined to the small, enclosed area of their flat. Her family seems to churn around and then past her, leaving her in a dim-lit, empty shell. Her husband casually hands her the newspaper on his way out and his work at the factory is something she remains ignorant about. She spends all her time on the balcony, smoking and looking at the sea. It seems to her that her entire life is colored with the tints and tones of waiting.

In *Voices in the City*, the boundaries of Monisha's life shrink with marriage. Her tasks are petty ones like cutting vegetables, serving food and brushing small children's hair. She rarely sees anyone outside the family and once her brother recovers from his illness she is even denied the privilege of driving out to see him. Confined lives tend to atrophy. As each day of her fractured, starved, cloistered existence passes, Monisha grows more of a "shrunken, etiolated, wasted thing" (*VC* 139). "I grow smaller every day," she reflects, "I will be invisible yet" (*VC* 139). Just prior to her suicide, she meditates, "...what a waste it has been, this life enclosed in a locked container" (*VC* 240). Immanence and inwardness are also characteristic of Maya's existence in *Cry, The Peacock*. Maya's background has not equipped her to engage in independent, productive activity. Her confined, limited life is reflected in the imagery of animals deprived of their freedom, like the caged monkeys on the railway platform and the bear deprived by its trainer of the freedom of the Himalayan forests. Another feature which sometimes characterizes the situation of the married woman, and which is reflected in the novels, is the lack of privacy. In *Voices in the City,* Anita Desai projects through Monisha the experience of a married woman within a joint family set-up. Monisha thinks wistfully of Jiban's last posting away from the family, where they had a house to themselves. She wishes she would be assigned household tasks which she could do away from the aunts, uncles, cousins, nieces and nephews. She feels she could work better this way and would feel more whole. However, privacy increasingly becomes a rarity. The reasons why Monisha cannot have a baby are discussed openly. It is as if her insides are "laid open, laid bare for their scrutiny" (*VC* 113). The room she and Jiban share, originally regarded as bridal, is soon invaded by the sisters-in-law who lie across the four-poster. They throw open her wardrobe to inspect her saris, while she wishes they would leave her alone, sometimes, to read. In her position as daughter-in-law, she merits no privacy with regard to visitors.

When Amla visits her, she is merely shown up to the mother-in-law's balcony and Monisha is brought there to meet her. The entire visit passes without a moment in which the sisters are left alone. Virginia Woolf point out that it is essential for a woman to possess privacy if she is to be able to write (Virginia Woolf 6). Anita Desai, referring to Virginia Woolf's eloquent plea in her own essay on "Women Writers", reiterates this necessity. Anita Desai says that a woman may be able to embroider an antimacassar sitting on a string-bed with a gaggle of sisters and aunts. She may even be able to paint a water-colour with her mother-in-law, grandmother, servants and infants watching her, but would not be able to write (Anita Desai 40). The need for privacy, one can definitely asset, applies not only to women writers but to women as a whole. In *Clear Light of Day,* Bim walking alone in the garden hears Tara calling to her. She wishes at that moment that she could be left alone to mutter to herself and behave like the solitary old woman she is, not as a sister or an aunt. She realizes then that perhaps privacy was what Mira-masi had needed and missed: they had never allowed her to be alone, never stopped pursuing her and surrounding her for a minute (*CL* 173).

In *Fire on the Mountain*, the lack of privacy an Indian woman with a large family experiences is seen in the case of Nanda Kaul. In the past, she would make an attempt at having a siesta every afternoon. However, he presence of others would intrude, until at 4 o'clock she would rise, sighing to herself, "all right. Come all of you, get me, I'm yours, yours again" (*FM* 24). Privacy, however, is a luxury which only the upper classes can afford. What about the married woman from the poorer sections of Indian society, living with a horde of children in crowded quarters? Sita and Maya can afford to loll around most of the day in complete privacy. Privacy may also bring with it its own problems. Many women feel their lot would improve if they were financially better off. However, with servants to do the work, a major curse may be boredom. The woman is all the more likely to feel herself living in a vacuum, shut up within the circle of herself. This is the case with Maya in *Cry, The Peacock* and Sita in *Where Shall We Go This Summer?*. On the whole, however, the need for privacy in a married woman's life, which Anita Desai focuses on in her novels, is a very real one. Another aspect of the Indian woman's married life is that, having often not pursued her education for long, her life becomes all the more limited. Anita Desai points out how the less educated a woman is, the less the printed word will signify to her. The Indian woman's spare time is preoccupied with inner preparation towards proving herself worthy to the requirements of her husband. She has no space of her in the home and society.

Motherhood: The Supreme Fulfilment

In the Indian context, a woman more or less proves herself through her ability to bear children. In *Voices in the City,*

Monisha is regarded as less of a woman because she is unable to give birth. Prior to her suicide, Monisha's sense of alienation deepens. She realizes that she will always be something of an outsider to her in-laws. This is partly because she does not share in their experience of maternity—there will always be "this sheet of glass, of metal between us," she thinks, "I have not given birth, I have not attended death" (*VC* 240). There is a common notion that something like a natural maternal instinct exists, and that a woman fulfils herself most completely in answering this instinct. A social and artificial morality is hidden behind this pseudo-naturalism. That the child is the supreme aim of the woman is a statement having precisely the value of an advertising slogan (Simone de Beauvoir, 538).

The truth is that there are as many diverse and variable reactions to motherhood as there are women. In India, social conditioning precludes the admission of attitudes divergent from the so-called norm. Women experience a strong sense of guilt in admitting even to themselves, that motherhood may not be as totally satisfying as it is made out to be.

What one appreciates in Anita Desai is that she allows for the possibility of attitudes totally opposite to conventional ones. In *Where Shall We Go This Summer?*, Sita's husband Raman thinks with conventional distaste, that it does not to be some her to react with paranoiac rage, fear and revolt to her fifth pregnancy. He hopes she will soon fill into the comfortable frame of large, placid joy supposed to go with pregnancy and parturition. When Sita tells him that she is not pleased, but frightened about her pregnancy, he says, "I thought it grows easier and easier." "It's not easier. It's harder-harder. It's unbearable," she weeps in reply (*WSGS* 32). Therefore, contrary to the conventional idea that women welcome the prospects of pregnancy and motherhood, Anita Desai registers the possibility of the Indian women experiencing variant and quite negative feelings towards them. Also, in India, with the unhygienic conditions which prevail in most hospitals and the inhuman indifference of medical staff, the whole experience of childbirth may prove to be a traumatic one, which many women wouldn't really care to repeat. Sita, for instance, visualizes the expressionless faces of the nurses in the gynecology ward "bored by yet another woman's panic-stricken labour" (*WSGS* 154).

Similarly, in *Fire on the Mountain,* thinks back on her many confinements, some in great discomfort at home, others at a small, filthy, missionary-run hospital and the nurses and doctors who could never quite help her out. Social attitudes also, expect motherhood to inspire feelings of unmitigated jove, pride and joy in the woman. Anita Desai, on the other hand, exposes the fact that a woman's attitude to her children may not be uniformly positive. Feelings of irritation, resentment and bitterness may also form part of the totality of her response to them.

Raman in *Where Shall We Go This Summer?* expresses conventional shock at the fact that Sita's happiest memory is not of her own home or children, but of strangers in a part. Sita murmurs in response: "Children?"..."children only mean anxiety, concern *pessimism* not happiness. What other women call happiness is just—just sentimentality" (*WSGS* 147). Nanda Kaul also serves to illustrate the fact that motherhood does not always evoke positive feelings. Reading her daughter's letter which begins with "Darling Mama", she can scarcely believe that there had been a time when she was actually addressed as such and had heart it quite naturally and calmly. It is not with any great pleasure that she remembers the years of being a mother of young children. To her, motherhood signifies seemingly endless duties. She recalls the chaos of teatime, or how one child would tumble off the swing, another would be stung by a wasp, a third would be slapped by a fourth and she would bend over them with that "ironic bow to duty that no one had noticed or defined" (*FM* 19). The wails which rip the house to pieces and the clutter make motherhood resemble a "noose" to her more than anything else.

Conclusion

Anita Desai is one of the epoch-making Indian women novelists. Her fictional world is replete with the incidental women's issues dormant deep in the Indian society. Her women represent varied types of womanhood—housewives, working women, concubines, social workers, and prostitutes. Desai has successfully depicted the woman's emotional, psychological, and physical predicament as if a stumbling block in her growth and development. She shows that the woman in India has her existence meaningful only in relation to the man she chooses or compelled to choose as her husband. All her hopes and aspirations are centeredaround the status and position of the man. She is not a part of the decision-making on both the domestic and social fronts. She senses a sense of alienation in her own world. The patriarchal set up has cut her off the mainstream. Anita Desai through her novels has artistically attempted bold, rebellious women characters who cross the magical margin and raise a battle against the cramping creeds and customs. Maya goes to the extent of murdering her mismatched husband.

One other striking issue which Desai has strikingly sensitized is the motherhood viewed as supreme fulfilment of the woman's life. The woman in Indian social context is still affected by the notion of womanhood. She remains incomplete if fails to give birth. She becomes target of hatred and discontent. She suffers from emotional handicap. Anita Desai, in her *Where Shall We Go This Summer?* has countered this issue. She implies the possibility of the Indian woman experiencing variant and quite negative feelings towards such social notions.

WORKS CITED

Amudra, Lop. "The Plight of Widows: Hiatus between Law and Social Acceptance", *Social Welfare: Focus on Women*, Vol. 29, No. 11-12 (February-March 1983).

Baig, Tara Ali. "A Zen for Men", *The Times of India Sunday Review*, 8 April 1984.

Beauvoir, Simone de. *The Second Sex*, Penguin Books, 1977.

Belliappa, Meena. *Anita Desai: A Study of Her Fiction*. Calcutta: Writers Workshop, 1977.

Desai, Anita. *Clear Light of Day*, New Delhi: Bombay, Calcutta, Madras, Bangalore, Hyderabad: Allied Publishers Private Limited, 1980 (reference to this edition of the novel, as *CL*).

Desai, Anita. *Cry, The Peacock*. Orient Paperbacks, New Delhi, 2001 (references to this abbreviated as *CP*).

Desai, Anita. *Fire on the Mountain* (Penguin Books, 1982), 138 (henceforth have reference to this edition of the novel, abbreviated as *FM*).

Desai, Anita. *Voices in the City*, New Delhi: Orient Paperbacks, 1982. All pages numbers quoted henceforth have reference to this edition of the novel, abbreviated as *VC*.

Desai, Anita. *Where Shall We Go This Summer?*, Vikas Publishing House, Delhi, 1975 (References as *WSGS*).

Desai, Anita. "Women Writers", Quest No. 65 (April-June 1970).

Dhawan, R.K. *Indian Women Novelists*, Set I: Vol. II. New Delhi: Prestige Books, 1991.

Gopal, N.R. *A Critical Study of the Novels of Anita Desai*. New Delhi: Atlantic Publishers, 1995.

Halperin, John. *The Theory of the Novel*. New York: Oxford University Press, 1947.

Iyengar, K.R. Srinivasa. *Indian Writing in English*. Sterling Publishers Pvt. Ltd., New Delhi, 1985.

Iyengar, K.R. Srinivasa. "A Note on Anita Desai's Novels", *The Banasthali Patrika,* No. 12 (January 1969).

Iyengar, K.R. Srinivasa. "Maya learns from him the meaning of pain, the habit of reflection." *The Banasthali Patrika,* No. 12 (January 1969).

Jain, Jasbir. *Anita Desai, Indian English Novelists: An Anthology of Critical Essays* (New Delhi-Bangalore-Jullundur: Sterling Publishers, Pvt. Ltd., 1982).

Parshley, H.M. *Preface to The Second Sex by Simone de Beauvoir,* Penguin Books, 1977.

Piciucco, Pier Paolo. *A Companion to Indian Fiction in English*. New Delhi: Atlantic Publisher & Distributors, 2004.

Shantha, Krishnaswamy. *The Women in Indian Fiction in English*. Ashish Publishing House, New Delhi, 1984.

Sharma, R.S. *Anita Desai,* New Delhi: Arnold Heinemann, 1981.

Sree, Prasanna. *Indian Women Writing in English: New Perspectives*. New Delhi: Sarup & Sons, 2005.

Sunwani, V.K. "Carignano—A Quiet Place", *Journal of Literary Studies*, Vol. 2, No. 2 (December 1979).

Vinson, James. *Contemporary Novelists*, London: St. James Press, 1972.

Woolf, Virginia. *A Room of One's Own*, London: Published by Leonard and Virginia Woolf at the Hogarth Press, 1935.

2

Love of Life in the Fiction of Anita Desai

Pushpa Lakhdive

Twentieth century has witnessed many changes in Indian literature in English especially because of the arrival of many women writers. Their presence has deeply influenced Indian fiction. According to Susie Tharu, "These writers contested the structures that were shaping their world. They tactically redeployed dominant discourses, held on to older strains, and recharged them with new meanings and even introduced new issues and new emphasis, new orientations." Though Toru Dutt, with her 'Bianca' introduced herself as an Indo-Anglian woman novelist, only after the Second World War women novelists of quality have begun enriching Indian fiction in English. Anita Desai, Kamala Markandaya, Ruth Jhabvala and Nayantara Sahgal are considered to be as significant novelists as Mulk Raj Anand, Raja Rao and R.K. Narayan. Along with these major figures, there are some other women novelists with an impressive corpus of fiction to their credit.

Anita Desai is one of the world famous and of India's best modern novelists in English. She is a writer who has influenced generations of writers. She has enriched Indian fictional world with her significant literary outputs. Anita Desai is able to narrate the story, to portray the characters, to convey the mood, to evoke the atmosphere, to probe the psyche of her characters successfully and for this she uses flashback technique, stream of consciousness technique, use of contrasting characters, use of symbolism and effective use of language either to evoke an atmosphere or the characters or to use rhetorical skill for harangue. And to create realistic effect she also uses Hindi words but in moderation.

Anita Desai, the best artistic author, has endeavored to accommodate the native Indian tradition in English language. Mainly, she portrays dilemmas and doubts of woman who are—misfits in their own way, who do not want to be heroic but all the time we find them struggling for what they do not have, for example love, affection, attention, acceptance, recognition, or appreciation. Her novel focuses on the inner climate, the climate of sensibility. The interplay of thoughts, feelings and emotions is reflected in language, syntax and imagery aspects of existentialism are in evidence in the total framework of her stories.

In this article, a modest attempt has been made to study love of life reflected in her novels with reference to three novels—*Cry, The Peacock*, *Voices in the City*, *Fire on the Mountain.*

Anita Desai's contribution to fiction writing has been quite commendable and substantial. She has added a new dimension to the Indian English fiction. She comes face-to-face with the intangible realities of life, the innermost depths of the human psyche and the chaotic underworld of human mind through her novels.

The world of Desai's fiction is largely a domestic one. She is interested primarily in the lives of women in India, rather than the history or politics of the subcontinent.

Desai's protagonists are not grand tragic heroes like that of Shakespeare. They are generally neurotic females, highly sensitive, sequestered in a world of dreams and imagination and alienated from their surroundings as a consequence of their failure or unwillingness to adjust with reality. They often differ in their opinion from others and embark on a lone voyage of contemplation in order to find the meaning of their existence. Their struggle is not some 'Evil' in their personality, but the nature to fight with existing reality, is the integral part of their personality.

Anita Desai is, of course, not blind to the immense possibilities of existence and to the problem of the relationship of art with life. Writing is, in fact, an act of faith, amoral necessity. By caring about the people whom he fictionalizes, the writer manifests his belief in the existence of others and this "caring or believing or love alone matters" and constitutes the writer's commitment to life. The Indian writers like Ruth Prawer Jhabvala, Kamala Markandaya, Nayantara Sahgal, Anita Desai, Namita Gokhale and Dina Mehta, in their portrayal of social scenario of Indian life have not lost sight of the seamy and somber realities operating underneath the facade of respectability. In spite of their delineation, of sordidness and seediness of the complex modern life, they do not side negativism. Desai's protagonists fruitlessly strive for the meaningful life, but they do not deny life. Whatever life they have as their lot, they try to mould it as per their ideals because they love life intensely.

The quest for life and love and the constant awareness of sorrow and death find repeated counterpointing in Desai's novels. Though she is aware of the miseries in human life, she is not blind towards the joys of life. Her interest in life is reflected in her setting, symbolism, and in the description of nature. These images are employed to reveal the inner nature and response of her characters and illuminate their love of life, obsessions, changing moods and aberrations. So these aspects will be studied to reveal her character's love of life.

Only the man who believes truly hopes, and only whoever truly hopes believes. We only believe what we hope, and hope what we believe. Hope, as a feeling, becomes the criterion by which the will casts under scrutiny the opposing forces of the tragic sense.

She thinks that the nature of human beings depends on their sentiments. Through such sentiments and feelings of Anita Desai's characters, their response to life is being studied. Their feelings reveal their 'true nature'. It seems that they desire intensely to live their life despite tragic sufferings.

Her characterization also reveals her keen love of life. Her attitude is not nihilistic. Most of her protagonists are females who embody in them the passion for life in spite of its wretchedness. Her characters Maya, Monisha, Sita, Nanda Kaul, Sarah, Bim, Sophie and Uma all are sensitive. They do not consider life to be an aimless, purposeless thing. They intuitively see special ends and therefore will this life despite its dust and dullness. They respond to life intensely.

Anita Desai gives importance to her protagonist's sensitiveness, feelings and emotions. Anita Desai explores their unconscious mind most artistically using symbols and images. Her characters are generally neurotic females, highly sensitive and alienated from their surroundings. Coming to her themes, Anita Desai seems to be quietly sliding in her scenes, settings and characters without much of an advance preparation. In fact, in her fiction, life is depicted as it really is. In her world, action is subordinated to psychology. In this respect, the novelist shows close affinity with Virginia Woolf who also entered the consciousness of the characters. These qualities of her contribute a lot to understand how she has attained remarkable success as a novelist.

The unconscious which Anita Desai explores has roots in our instincts, our impulses, and in our desires and not in our mental fixation of the Freudian mould. Out of this unconscious springs, the affinities of love, the thrills of beauty and ecstasies of mystical and religious experiences. Anita Desai considers her characters as living individuals of 'flesh and bone'. They are not case studies of neurosis, nor are they evolutionary histories of Psychological Phenomenon. They are sensitive individuals interested in life with its hopes, dejections, and chaotic flow. They are moved by the aesthetics of existence.

The inherent misery of human conditions does not blind Anita Desai to the joys of life. Her love of life reveals through her characters, in the beautiful description of nature in the response of her characters to the nature, and also in their response to life.

All female protagonists in Anita Desai's novels have the passion for life in spite of its wretchedness. It is not that men in Anita Desai's novels have lost love for life, but they like Gautama and Raman as their very names suggest have paradoxically disinterested interest in life. On the contrary, Maya and Sita do not consider life to be an aimless, purposeless thing as their counterpart do; they intuitively see special ends and therefore will this life despite its dust and dullness.

The moments of revelation of life come in an aesthetic experience, such as in the manifestation of natural beauty as 'In custody' when the sky fills in with a gray light and the pampas grass.

"Waved in a sudden breeze that had sprung up, laughing, waving and rustling through the grasses with a live, rippling sound." Being a psychological novelist, Anita Desai deals with internal states of minds of her characters. She therefore employs the language of thoughts and interior selves of her characters. This language of the interior is best communicated through images, symbols, and myths. It is therefore not surprising that Anita Desai's novels abound in rich and symbolic images of light and colour, of the sun, the moon, stars, storm, river, sea, birds, insects and animals. These images are employed to reveal her characters love of life, obsessions, changing moods and psychic aberrations.

Her heroines, like Maya live by their sense of touch, smell, sight, and taste. In *Cry, The Peacock*, there is emotional alienation and temperamental gulf between Maya and Gautama. Maya's obsessive love of the beautiful, the colourful, the sensuous, and the picturesque in life stands in sharp contrast with Gautama's philosophical, detachment in life. Maya's world is "full". Her appetite for the "real, the close, the living" is insatiable. But Gautama, a thick-skinned creature, is unable to appreciate the pulsating richness of life. She remarks "Poor Gautama, Not to be able to notice the odour of limes...."

> The blossoms of the lemon tree were different, quite different of much stronger, crisper character, they seemed cut out of hard moon shells, by a sharp knife of mother-of-pearl into curving scimitar petals that guarded the heart of fragrance. Their scent, too, was more vivid, a sour astringent scent, refreshing as that of ground peel, a crushed lemon leaf.[1]

Thus, in *Cry, The Peacock*, the poetic and highly subjective descriptions of the outside world often indicate the state of mind of the character and invariably create the character. These highly sensuous descriptions symbolize Maya's intense love of life; the flowers, the lemons in all their concreteness convey much more powerfully than mere statement can, that obsessive love of life which makes Maya decide to murder her husband. The loving visions of the world of nature suggest a sensibility clinging to the beautiful and picturesque things of life. Language reveals character.

Maya's love of the picturesque and the colourful is connected with her keen interest in life. Her language is the language of the flowers and fruits, of sunrises and sunsets, of the dance of the peacock and the flutter of the butterfly.

What Maya longs for is the life principle. She cries for life here and now, a life of rich satisfaction, of style. She loves blue twilight in the garden vibrated with exotic poetic words like 'Zulph' and 'Mehtab' in the accompaniment of twisting of 'Paimana'.

Nature is a familiar presence in Anita Desai's novels. Her love for and obsession with nature is deep-seated force that moulds her vision. "Nature provides her novels an exotic touch and colourful texture. It also helps in dissolving the dark gloom which envelopes her fiction."

Cry, The Peacock begins with "gentle bees", "unthinking butterflies", and "the bougain villaea-coloured evening air". Maya's garden has a large variety of exotic flowers. Desai describes her garden beautifully.

"There were still some beds of petunias floppy white and faint mauve petunias, sentimental, irresolute flowers, I always felt, and yet at-dust, they admitted such a piercing swoon of scent, poignant, half-sweet, half-sad fragrance that matched my mood to perfection, and I started to it with the embrace of recognition, taking in deep breaths of this gentle, fading odour that was so laden with wistful remembrance of the winter, a sense of all good things having come to an end, and only the long, weary summer to look forward to...".[2] The poetical description of spring reflects the spring in Maya's mind:

> Down the street the silk-cotton trees were the first to flower; their huge scarlet blooms thick-petaled, solid-podded that made blood blobs in the blue, then dropped to the asphalt and were squashed into soft, yellowish miasma...so, heavy,

> so moist and living to the touch. Their pods were clouded with silk-cotton, and they burst, these airy faery puffs of silver-streaks whiteness were released and sailed through the air like angelic, soft-feathered birds, and rolled along the streets in radiant billow tree the dust soiled them.[3]

Maya who is the main character in the novel admits that she rejoices "in the world of sounds, senses, movements, odours, colours and tunes". The title of the novel is deeply symbolical. The cries, calls animating of peacocks evoke frenzied picture of Maya's anguish and restlessness. The dance of peacocks is a mix of bliss and agony:

> How they stamp their feet, and beat their beaks against the rocks. They will even grasp the snakes that live on the sands there, and break their bodies to bits against the stones, to ease their own pain. Before they mate they fight. They will rip each other's breasts to strips and fall, bleeding, with their beaks open and panting.[4]

Maya longs for contact and relationship with Gautama. Love may be the best possible way to find salvation for the sages, but for those, who are "human beings of flesh and bone" it is the basis and true cause of their existence.

She realized that it is not only for Gautama's presence that she longs for but mainly for the life that would permit her to touch him, feel his flesh and hair, and then tighten her hold on him.

Anita Desai establishes an identity between setting and the mental state of Maya, in order to show her desire to live and love. As Maya is a woman with powerful emotions and feelings, she wants love in every form. She wants physical union as well as mental union. That Maya wants a sexual union is clearly perceptive in her contemplation and exultation on seeing the male and female papaya trees in the garden. The description is richly erotic:

> I contemplated that, smiling with pleasure at the thought of those long streamers of bridal flowers that flow out of the core of the female papaya tree and twine about her slim trunk, and the firm, wax-petalled blossoms that leap directly out of the solid trunk of the male.... Besides, if I

> could pleasure in contemplation of the male papaya, how much more food for delight in this male companion, surely.[5]

Maya frequently indulges in egoistic fantasies. In her world of imagination, she is the main centre. It fulfils her need for total attention and importance. The perfect and ideal love which Maya aspires for exists only in her make-believe world or the world of nature. She prefers the world of flowers, and trees, birds and blooms, because in them she finds no contradiction of her thoughts and feelings. Maya wants her husband to take care of her, like a delicate flower "so as not to bruise it". Such thoughts provide her security and piece: "yes, I murmured, 'yes' caressing the flower, feeling the grass, pickle, feeling security lap me, safety and piece. A lovely vision was being created for me, and I half closed my eyes and dreamt." It is a world full of beauty and passion. Watching a butterfly flicker amongst the flowers, she forgets her despair and imagines: "The world is like a toy specially made for me, painted in my favourite colours set moving to my favourite tunes." When Gautama pulls her up for her absorption in a world of fairy tales, she tells him: "I don't care to detach myself into any other world than this. It isn't boring for me.... The world is full-full, Gautama."

In Gautama's family, the atmosphere is heavily charged with intellectual, social and political discussions. Here "one did not speak of love far less of affection". Maya cannot participate in their ceaseless and heated debates. Maya cannot, by temperament and training is one with her in-laws. To give her life a meaning and to save herself from self-hate, she holds on to her identity. In chapter one of part II, she also remarks that murders are committed "only for the sake of money, or property, or anything solid, and dirty; not for love, or life or basic things". It reveals her intense love of life that prompts her to kill her husband.

In *Cry, The Peacock*, the husband-wife relationship serves to show two different approaches to life, Maya lives intensely. Gautama is remote detached, intellectual, sane, prosaic really. Maya, in spite of its painful affairs, believes in involvement; while Gautama preaches detachment a life like 'lily and lotus'.

She wants to live and love and for that she is prepared to die and not perish on the dead branch of detachment. Maya is sensitive and high strung, while Gautama is rational. Gautama believed in guiding the body with the dictates of the mind. He considers Maya's romantic view of love as criminal. He urges her to detach herself from a personal world she has created around herself and implores her to create a real world instead to attach herself with. Maya however remains unconvinced. She insistently replies:

> I don't care to detach myself into any other world than this. It isn't boring for me never boring. I suppose I get much more of it than you do. Could you, sit here, on the steeps without a book, without a piece of paper even, just looking at the trees and thinking about 'them'?

And Gautama fails to sip life drop by drop as Maya sips it. When he replies in negative, she powerfully expresses her longing of life in this reply:

> But, you see, I can, I have so much to look at, to touch, and feel, and be happy about. I like to walk about here and touch things—leaves, sticks, earth, everything. I play with my cat. And if I am lonely, I can visit my friends.
>
> The world is full-full, Gautama. Do you know what that means? I am not bored with it that I should need to hunt another one![6]

In short, she refutes the argument that it is an empty world as it appears to the analytical mind of Gautama.

There is a temperamental gulf between Maya and Gautama. Gautama, who touches without feeling, and Maya, who feels even without touching. A slight touch of his fingers brings out spontaneous reaction of joy to her:

> Fall, fall, long fall into the primordium of original instinct, of first formed love.

Gautama's theories nevertheless appear to her as sound as a mass of rock in the middle of a tossing sea. To hold to it is safety, she feels. To be borne away from it, by her insane passion is to perish. Maya cannot help but perish. She has not allowed the springs of her life to go dry by the shallow rationalism of Gautama.

The albino the Kathakali dance, the peacocks, the bronze Shiva and her own pounding heart symbolize the longing to live to the last dregs of satisfaction.

The symbol of Nataraja reinforces Maya's love of life. She feels that she has a greater justification to live. She feels, "Gautama had never lived, and never would."

At times the extravagance of her sensuousness becomes somewhat oppressive, Maya's 'love with living' juxtaposed with the awareness that there is "only death and waiting" is suggested, moreover, through the explicit symbolism of the peacock. The dance of the peacocks:

> They spread out their splendid tails and began to dance, but like Shiva's this dance of joy is the dance of death, and they dance, knowing that they and their lovers are all to die, perhaps, even before the monsoons come to an end.... Living they are aware of death. Dying they are in love with life. "lover, lover" you will hear them crying in the forests, when the rain clouds come, "Lover, I die".[7]

Symbolically, it suggests Maya's love of life and obsession with death which lead her to the final crack-up. Maya's burning longing to live and her fore-knowledge of death makes her life the last song of a swan and the mating of peacocks.

Though haunted by the fear of death, Maya is full of sensuous love for life and preservation of life. She is fully alive and responds to the varying moods of nature and its charm. She cannot bear death or cruelty in any form.

Toto's death shatters her completely. Once at the sight of cage upon cage of monkeys at the railway station, she starts crying saying, "there's not even a bowl of water for them...and those cages are too small to contain their bodies". And Gautama coolly tells her that those monkeys were being sent abroad for experimental purposes.

She longs for a passionate contact not only with Gautama but with the pulsating world around her—from the stars in the sky to the owls on the fig tree—all that suggest life.

In *Cry, The Peacock*, sudden and unexpected and breathtakingly beautiful glimpses into something new are frequently offered.

The fleeting glimpse of a "dark young woman in a crimson sari holding a white dog on the leash walk into a sheltered house followed by a dark young man in white".

The laughter that gurgles up Maya's throat "as I saw a goat nuzzle secretly a basket of sliced melon in the bazaar while the vendor's back was turned" offer teasing glimpses into unknown aspects of everyday life. They add to the richness of the texture of the novel. These examples may be viewed simply as beautiful passages which offer additional pleasure. But they are not merely decorative passages. Apart from offering teasing glimpses evoking vast areas of suggestion, they are all functional. They symbolise the insatiable appetite for life of Maya. It is this tremblingly sensitive response to the richness of life that makes Maya commits murder.

Maya is a sensitive and imaginative girl who asks questions of life and seeks to elicit meaning from experience. Beauty, evil mortality haunts her mind till the end. It is her failure to control experience that results in vanity. She cannot accommodate her tumultuous responses to available patterns of living. Nor is she equal to sustaining an individual quest for meaning.

The awareness of a confusing duality of existence conveyed through a recurrent colour, symbolism. Maya's consciousness hovers round a particular colour, which gets translated into different sensations under varying conditions. Red for instance is Maya's colour. Her hunger, for the coloured and alive world is seen in her fascination for red manifesting itself in numerous objects—ruby red as red roses, red wine, mandarin oranges, gul-mohur, red melon, scarlet-striped kites, red bangles, etc.

Maya's experience of love is not of ecstasy that is short lived, but of ecstasy that is never attained. Maya loves life desperately, though life seems to her only sufferings. Though Maya's life does not give her happiness and as a painful struggle, yet she has not the nihilistic attitude towards life. She is against the denial of life. Her response to the richness of life is acute.

The nature and the natural environment are the material on which Anita Desai weaves her tragic tales. Nature is a familiar presence in Desai's novels. Natural landscape fuses with the character's inner milieu and provides a new dimension to her view of nature. Her love for and obsession with nature is not superficial. It is deep-seated in her mental make up and is part of a large vision which guides her novels in the stark barren and lifeless lives of the protagonists. Nature acts both, as a metaphor of hope and life and as an ironical presence that sharpens the awareness of a grim existence.

Voices in the City presents a touching account of the unhappy, loveless life of Monisha, the married sister of Nirode. The environment in which Anita Desai's characters are condemned to live once again has a crucial role to play. The sordidness, the brutality, and the sheer dreariness of the physical world is the force that her characters revolt against. The three main characters of the book are rebels. They see more than the others; they see through appearances at the dreariness of everyday life. They feel more than the others. The ugly physical reality, for them, is both a fact and a symbol—symbolic of an attitude and of a value that they cannot accept while in *Cry, The Peacock* the outside world is used to reflect the state of mind of the main character, in *Voices in the City* it has much more positive role to play. It is one of the characters in the novel, the most powerful. It is the antagonist whom Monisha, Nirode and Emm confront every moment of their lives.

Monisha is in sharp contrast with Maya. Maya craves for contact, relatedness, communication. Monisha being secretive by nature loves isolation. There is no life giving rapport between Monisha and Jiban. In the overpopulated and suffocating household in Bow Bazar, she does not get time to be near Jiban, or pines for an opportunity to share her joys and sorrows with him. She feels nostalgic about Jiban's last posting out in a district, away from the city and the family...not because there she enjoyed the affable company of her husband, but because of the solitude there which she, like her brother, Nirode, regards her sole natural condition. Monisha feels that the garden of Kalimpong is her abode of peace. She is delighted by the solitude of the jungles;

the aqueous shadows of the bamboo groves and the earth lay with great fallen leaves:

> The solitude of the jungles there, the aqueous shadows of the bamboo groves and the earth laid with great fallen leaves.... Jiban away on tour, I alone with myself, no visitors at all. Our house which we had to ourselves, its room almost bare of furniture, its squares of empty space and silence—friends to me, and I've had to leave them behind.[8]

This is in sharp contrast with the dark, gloomy existence she leads in her in-laws house in Calcutta. Monisha draws a distinct line between her and the joint family "ever sleeps out under the stars at night. They have indoor minds, starless and darkless."

Monisha revolts against the darkness of the city, Calcutta since it denies access to the other darkness she seeks between the stars:

> I'll have only the darkness. Only the dark-spaces between the stars, for they are the only things on earth that can comfort me, rub a balm into my wounds, into my throbbing head, and bring me this coolness, this stillness, this interval of peace.[9]

Thus, Monisha longs for these type of "few moments of night silence". She wants privacy in her crowded family and in overcrowded city. Though there is all-pervasive darkness in her life, she has interest in life. She wants some moment that will give her privacy; it may be the darkness of night. Her interest in singing and music suggests her interest in the life-song too. There is a reference to her singing in her diary. "A little more cheerful, is she? Sniffs Jiban's mother when she hears me singing to Kalyani di's baby in its cradle that hangs from the rafters." When she has been sent to a concert of music, she becomes one with the musical notes of sitar. She writes:

> Then the sitar player comes out to play.... As a blessing upon my trust, he pours his music down upon me.... To each note my every vein and artery responds like a taut, sweet sitar string, "plucked by my own emotions that match his faultlessly".

She thinks of the street singer's emotions that 'spread through her eyes like dark lakes', as she fears they would dissolve and her into a meaningless shadow.

The domestic tasks, like cutting vegetables, serving food, brushing small children's hair are assigned to Monisha. She does not mind doing all this, but longs for something which can be done alone in privacy, Anita Desai rightly employs a device like Diary to expose Monisha's prattle. Monisha says:

> Only I wish I were given some tasks I could do alone, in privacy, away from the aunts and uncles, the cousins and nieces and nephews. Alone I could work better, and I should feel more—whole. But less and less there is privacy. Even my own room, which hey regarded at first as still bridal, now no longer is so...the whole wardrobe full of books. To my perplexity she laughs. I am no longer perplexed. I see that of course she cannot know that there is nothing to laugh at in Kafka or Hopkins or Dostoevsky or my Russian or French or Sanskrit dictionaries. But I wish they could live me alone, sometime to read.[10]

Her love of life reflects in her fondness of reading and silence. But she is largely miserable because she does not have what she longs.

Thus, Monisha seeks life in privacy. Monisha's diary throws light on her love for nature. She enjoyed the days, away from Calcutta and the joint family, near Kalimpong and "The solitude of the jungles there, the aqueous shadows of the bamboo groves and the earth laid with great leaves. The bell like dignity, of the elephant on whom we rode through the jungles."[11]

Monisha likes reading books. Her fondness of reading and silence reflects her response towards life. She loves life most. She wants to live life on her own way. But she is largely miserable because she does not have any privacy. Monisha is destitute of the vital element of love. Her equation with Jiban is also devoid of genuine love. She feels alienated from her husband and ponders over the problems of attachment and detachment. Monisha is fond of the *Gita*. My book *She* calls it *Gita* inspires her to be detached because from attachment arises longing.... It only love existed that is not binding, that is free of rules, obligations, complicity and all stirrings of mind or conscience, then but there is no such love.

It is significant that Monisha commits suicide out of despair at not being able to experience life and not because she has not love for life. Her suicide, the very act of death, points out her triumph over life. Her suicide is an attempt to find out meaning in her existence.

Almost all the images of the city in *Voices in the City* are those of oppression, of decay, and of death. But there are some images wherein lurks writer's love of life, other images, like that; of the kite, or of the river, represent a release from the metallic prison that the city has become:

> One must be a-king kite wheeling so far away in the blazing empty sky as to be merely a dot almost invisible to the urchins who stood below stone in their fists, ready to be aimed and flung.

Anita Desai has delineated two minor characters who are contrasted with the city and its misfits, represent a positive value. These are the painter Sharma with his mystery and wisdom, and the Irishman, Davy, an "unattached, drifting, bird-creature" with that, "Vital element of love," that is missing, in the three main characters. The Irishman Davy and Dharma, the painter, stand for peace and tranquility.

Though Anita Desai basically seems to be saying—the longer one lives the deeper he suffers the bitter assaults of existence, yet in her novels, the change to more positive attitude towards life is also noticeable. This might have been the result of her own changing attitude to life, running almost parallel to her own growth and maturity.

In her novel, *Fire on the Mountain*, Anita Desai's protagonist Nanda Kaul reflects her vision of life. Her love of life is manifested in the characterization of Nanda Kaul. Nanda Kaul is leading a life of isolation and feels happy at Carignano on the hillside. Her life as a Vice Chancellor's wife, though crowded and full of social activity was essentially meaningless and unsatisfying. She is an epitome of devotion, duty, and sacrifice. She hankers for love. But the revelation of the presence of another woman in her husband's life comes as a jolt to her. Under such circumstances also she does not give up life. This wisdom and courage show her sense of life. This shows her deep love of life.

Though Nanda Kaul gets so much humiliation, mental torture in her life, she does not end her life. This shows her deep love of life.

Nanda Kaul vacillates between two contradictory forces—withdrawal and involvement, detachment, and attachment, "the need to withdraw in order to preserve one's wholeness and sanity and the need to be involved in the painful process of life".

We meet Nanda Kaul at Carignano when she has lived her full life-span. Her life as a Vice Chancellor's wife, though crowded and full of social activity, was essentially meaningless and unsatisfying. She is an epitome of devotion, duty, and sacrifice. She hankers for love. But the revelation of the presence of another woman in her husband's life comes as a jolt to her. Thus, her busy schedule lacks warmth and understanding. Under such circumstances also she does not give up life. All her life, she lives there only because of her sense of duty towards others. This wisdom and courage show her sense of life. She fiercely desires absolute isolation and stillness even during her busy life, yet, she never shirks her responsibilities.

As if to relax her taut nerves, because of the unbearable, emotional strain, she practices stillness and composure, for years for an hour every afternoon: "it was an art not easily acquired". It was very difficult to get rest in that busy house where nothing was ever still:

> From all sides these sounds invaded her room which was in the centre.... This would go for an hour and she would keep her eyes tightly shut, her clenched hands folded on her chest...determinedly not responding. The effort not to respond would grow longer by the minute, heavier, more unbearable till at last it was sitting on her chest grasping her by the neck. At four O'clock she would break out from under with a gasp. All right she would say...come, come all of you, get me, I'm yours, yours again.[12]

Her capacity to accommodate others and sacrifice shows her deeply-rooted sense of responsibility. Till then she leads life as is expected of her.

After her husband's death, she wants to live life in her own style in Carignano. She feels happy in the barrenness and emptiness of the house.

"All she wanted was to be alone, to have Carignano to herself, in this period of her life when stillness and calm were all that she wishes to entertain."[13]

She wants no one and nothing else. This is not a denial of life but choice of a particular way of life that she cherishes so long. But Raka's arrival breaks her dreams of peace. Nanda Kaul's apprehensions that her privacy is once again going to be threatened by the presence of Raka are, however, soon allayed when she finds her great-granddaughter, a strange, isolated child whose own wish for solitude is as—intense as her own. Raka avoids communicating with her great-grandmother and spends most of her time in roaming.

> Like her own great-grandmother Raka wanted only one thing-to be left alone and pursue her own secret life amongst the rocks and pines of Kasauli.[14]

Nanda Kaul's isolation has been self-imposed. Raka is recluse by nature. It hurts Nanda Kaul to find herself neglected by her own great-granddaughter. She wants to establish a viable rapport with the child wheats recluse by nature. In fact, her instinct nature is to love and to be loved. As R.S. Sharma observes, at Carignano she deliberately seeks to exclude what she needs most—the security and fulfillment of love.[15]

Nanda Kaul, in *Fire on the Mountain*, recasts her childhood fantasies not only to hold interest, of her great-granddaughter but "also to give herself the much needed feeling of significance. She wants to penetrate Raka's secret world. She offers to go for a walk with her and during this walk, there is a moment of shared laughter," a coming together as it were only to pull apart the moment the idea of pattern enters their conversation Raka's sense of the essential upsets Nanda Kaul; somehow Raka's withdrawal does not conform to the conventional idea of normalcy and Mrs. Kaul desires response from her. She seeks to fire her imagination, to hold her interest and in this process she endows her father with imaginary travels, travels which he had never undertaken, and with animals he had never kept. It is a world of private fantasy in which "she lives an escape, for after all nobody wanted the truth and no one could bear it. It is because reality is unbearable that she builds a protective wall of solitude, only to find that it is vulnerable and requires constant effort to be maintained.

Maternal love and her basic instinct to take care of others' nature weaken Nanda Kaul's self-imposed detachment. Once again she looks for someone to care for. Her inner dictates force her "to reach out to other," to love and be loved. Nanda is filled with tenderness for Raka instinctively. She wants to help the child in going bed and took her in.

> Habit would fear its head inside her, make her prepare to follow tell her to tuck the child in, read her a story and lead her safely into sleep.[16]

All along her life she has tried to feel wanted and loved. Consciously or unconsciously her efforts have been to get a positive response from her family for her devotion, but all in vain. Now she directs all her energies to win Raka despite all the betrayals and disappointments she received from a faithless husband and selfish children, she feels irresistibly drawn towards Raka because she desperately longs for love and realises that if she is discarded any longer she will be crushed by self-hate. The need to reclaim Raka's love indicates Nanda's unconscious longing to feel loved, her instinctive drive to life. That is why Nanda Kaul again gets involved in life.

Anita Desai uses significant imagery and symbols to convey her character's vision and attitude of life. The critic S. Indira sums up the significance of imagery in *Fire on the Mountain* quoting D.H. Lawrence and the novelist herself: "It is the charming mosaic of imagery woven so skillfully by the novelist that makes the Novel a work of art."[17] Quoting D.H. Lawrence who said "If I eat an apple, I like to eat it with my senses," Anita Desai herself stated that the novel in which she attempted this closeness of man and beast, earth and vegetable was *Fire on the Mountain.*

Another important aspect of this novel's narrative technique is its symbolism. There are several symbols that deepen the philosophic implications of the novel. Carignano is symbolic of the loneliness and barrenness of human life in general and Nanda Kaul in particular: What pleased and satisfied her so, here at Carignano, was its barrenness. This was the chief virtue of Kasauli, of course—its starkness.... Occasionally an eagle swam through this clear undoubted mass of light and air.

The lonely house is symbolic of the lonely life of Nanda Kaul and Raka. The barrenness and starkness associated with it symbolise an essential human condition alienation. The eagle symbol, like the house symbol, is repeatedly used in the course of the novel to highlight the aspect of quest, the quest for a meaning of life. The sight of the eagle flying high, makes Nanda long to be able to soar like the bird: "An eagle swept over...its wings outspread, gliding on currents of air without once moving its great muscular wings which remained in repose, in control, she [Nanda Kaul] had wished, it occurred to her, to imitate the eagle-gliding, with eyes closed."

As in other novels in *Fire on the Mountain* too Anita Desai uses poetry for the reflection of her characters' mind. This time it is a poem by Hopkins:

> I have desired to go
> Where springs not fail
> To fields where no sharp and sided hail
> And a few lilies below
> And I have asked to be
> Where no storms come,
> Where the green swell is in the havens dumb,
> And out of the swing to the sea.[18]

This poem has some connection with Nanda Kaul who quotes it and the poem signifies her desire to be away from the humdrum of life, to a heaven of nature far from the madding crowd. By introducing this poignant stanza from Hopkin's poem, Anita

Desai highlights the strong desire of Nanda Kaul to have a life of her own choice. She loves life.

Though Anita Desai basically seems to be saying—the longer one lives the deeper he suffers the bitter assaults of existence, yet in her novels, the change to more positive attitude towards life is also noticeable. This might have been the result of her own changing attitude to life, running almost parallel to her own growth and maturity.

Female protagonists Maya, Monisha, Nanda Kaul, Sita, Bim, Sarah, Sophie, Uma, crave for love and the meaning in life. They have intense love for life. But external forces threaten their longing for life, at times it is denied to them. This conflict between their love of life and the harsh real life creates severe inner crisis in their mind. Eventually, their mind crumbles down. The great force which affect tragically against their love of life is the incompatibility of husband-wife relation. This incompatibility results in a marital discord.

Thus, in spite of their sufferings, these characters love life intensely. With their highstrung sensitiveness, they desire to drink life to the last drop.

NOTES

1. Anita Desai (1963). *Cry, The Peacock*. rpt. Orient Paperbacks, New Delhi, 1988, 21.
2. *Ibid*., 18-19.
3. *Ibid*., 34.
4. *Ibid*., 35.
5. *Ibid*., 95.
6. *Ibid*., 117-18.
7. *Ibid*., 95-96.
8. Anita Desai (1965). *Voices in the City*. rpt. Orient Paperbacks, New Delhi, 1968, 116.
9. *Ibid*., 138.
10. *Ibid*., 115-16.
11. *Ibid*., 126.
12. Anita Desai (1977). *Fire on the Mountain*. Allied Publishers Pvt. Ltd., New Delhi 1985, 23.
13. *Ibid*., 17.

14. *Ibid.*, 48.
15. R.S. Shanna (1981). *Anita Desai*, Arnold Heinemarnn, New Delhi.
16. Anita Desai (1977). *Fire on the Mountain.* Allied Publishers Pvt. Ltd., New Delhi, 1985, 80.
17. S. Indira (1994). *Anita Desai as an Artist: A Study in Image and Symbol.* Creative Rooks, New Delhi.
18. Anita Desai (1977). *Fire on the Mountain.* Allied Publishers Pvt. Ltd., New Delhi, 1985, 58.

3

Women Sensibility in Select Novels of Mahasweta Devi

K. Radha and R. Rajalaksmi

Women write in a different way from men and they mainly write about themselves. Women writers write mainly to voice their anxiety for and sympathize with the suffering of the women. Being women themselves, they better understand the inner voice of a female rather than a male writer. The figure of women in fiction has undergone a transformation after all through the last four decades. Women writers have shifted away from customary portrayals of lasting, self-sacrificing women to divergent female characters searching for their identity, no longer characterized and defined in terms of their victim position. They are trying to expose the condition of women in society. Through their characters, they picture the real emotions and sensibility of a woman.

Mahasweta Devi is one of the famous Indian English writers who does not belong to the marginalized community; yet she speaks up for the poor people. In her novels, she brings out the sufferings of the Indian doubly marginalized women. She examines the various facets of a typical marginalized woman's birth, childhood, adulthood and life patterns. She mainly addresses the issues of exploitation and marginalization as long continuing socio-historical process embedded in social and cultural practices. She has also spread the consciousness of the necessity of struggle among the suppressed poor people for the attainment of their dignity and freedom. She draws an excellent portrayal of the character of women, the way they are exploited and their sufferings in the hands of the male world.

Among the Indian women writers, Mahasweta Devi is primarily concerned with the psychological crises in the lives of Indian women who are subjected to physical and psychological tortures in a male-dominated society in her novels. She has exploited her skill in projecting convincingly the agonized mind of the persecuted women. In her novels, she mainly focuses on the existential predicament and travails of the subdued women in a male-dominated society governed by rigid traditions and restricts. Being a woman, she dives deep into the inner mind and emotions of the repressed women by virtue of their feminine sensibility and psychological insight and bring to light the issues which are the outcome of their psychological and emotional imbalances.

One such writer is Mahasweta Devi who exposes the sensibility and sufferings of low-caste women in traditional Indian society. Women of India are the worst victims of male tyranny. They are assigned to inferior place as far as culture and tradition are concerned. A woman as is seen in terms of the male-oriented world, a world which identifies her from the male counterpart. She is gentle, dependent, emotional, submissive, sensitive, and sensible. Women belonging to the deprived communities face exploitation, subjugation, and subordination both from upper caste men and men of their own community. Such is the degrading conditions in which the low-caste woman is destined to live. Her acute and perceptive pen brings them to life with a deep empathy and sensitivity which makes these women to step out of the margins of society to live in their own minds, impressive in their quite courage and tenacity, their will to survive.

Almost all of Mahasweta Devi's female protagonists articulate the larger questions of the community of people who are erased from the discourses of mainstream fiction. Her stories are remarkable for their complete lack of sentimentality. The women characters in her works are stronger when compared to men. To uphold humanity Mahasweta Devi poured out her longings and anger in her works to awaken people from the bondage of meaningless old traditions and culture.

> I am a woman, and I am writing. But I am not writing of women alone. What I am writing...is about class exploitation. (Mahasweta Devi 42)

Sensibility emerged as a concept in the Enlightenment Era but continued to be defined during the Romantic Period and beyond. The term describes people's capacity to be affected by the world around them. It also directly correlates their emotional capabilities with their moral development. Since concepts such as piety, modesty, and obedience defined the moral standard for women, feminine sensibility required women to display such qualities in their behaviour. It also refers to the exaggerated expressions of emotions.

Sensibility reflects the sense of ability to feel or perceive. It also depicts the refined awareness and appreciation in matters of feeling. The sensibility or sensitiveness illustrates the quality or condition of being emotionally and intuitively sensitive. Women are well known for their sentiments, sensations, emotions, sensitiveness or sensitivity. Sensibility is an important 18th-century term assigning a kind of emotional response or receptiveness. It refers to a sensitive consciousness or attentiveness towards something such as the emotions of another. The consequences of not being trained to live sensibly are devastating. Without being sensible, *The Bible* says a beautiful woman will look like gross. A sensible woman thinks before she acts.

The word 'sensibility' points out the receptiveness of the senses and refers to the psycho-perceptual system. It indicates the function of the nervous system and the material basis for consciousness. Women sensibility means the sentiments of a woman, as it is her psychology or longing. On the whole, it is a kind of reaction towards action concerned with a woman's feeling and emotions to her own miseries and circumstances. Through sensibility we can recognize women's psychology and longing. Thus, women sensibility is the matter of soft and pure emotions of a woman's heart. The feelings which she stores in her heart have the capacity to overwhelm her surroundings. The sensibility has the depths of sea and heights of sky. In 1792, Mary Wollstonecraft defined sensibility in her work *A Vindication of the Rights of Woman* as, "Sensibility can be defined as cultivated emotion or the capacity for it; it includes spontaneous sympathy and exquisitely polished instinct" (78).

In our traditional Indian society, nobody tried to observe a woman's deep feeling or emotional response. She did not have any freedom to express her feelings and emotions. The sufferings of low-caste women are uncountable. They are abused and exploited as beasts. In general, the woman is reduced to a womb to be ruled and dominated by male laws. Her whole identity is erased and she becomes a mere reproductive machine. They are struggling to claim their individual status in a rigid patriarchal society, where she is sexually exploited and ruined. Women are not having any human rights to talk about their feelings and their dissatisfaction about destiny is of no account; she has been treated as a lower-caste. Women are not having any individuality throughout their life and they only have a shadowy existence.

> In childhood a woman should be under her father's control, in youth under her husband's, and when her husband is dead under her son's. She should not have independence. (*Manusmriti*, 5148)

In the novel *Mother of 1084,* Mahasweta Devi explores the psychological and emotional crises of married women in Hindu families. The novelist exposes the plight of the subaltern mother Sujata who live like encaged animals deprived of freedom and discretion. The neglected and suppressed plight of the women is represented by Sujata Chatterjee whose beloved son Brati Chatterjee was brutally murdered at the hands of the oppressive state machinery because of his involvement in the Naxalite movement. Brati was dissatisfied not only with the system prevalent in the country but was also frustrated at home where his mother was humiliated and suppressed by his father Dibyanath Chatterjee. Brati wanted her mother to fight against his father; but he refers to it in a gentle manner so as not to offend her delicate sensibility. Brati was indeed more sensitive than the others, and the most concerned about his mother's well-being. He articulated the feelings of frustration and sorrow that she had always kept repressed within her.

As soon as Dibyanath comes to know about the news of his son that he is lying dead in the police morgue, instead of running to the police station he tries to hush up the matter with the fear of stigma in the society. He was very quiet without any sympathy towards his son. Sujata is aghast to see the indifferent behaviour of her husband. The uncomprehending Sujata is set as a strong contrast to her materialistic husband, Dibyanath. She who stands with her hands tightly pressed to her mouth, a look of disbelief in her eyes. She hardly finds any sympathetic members of the house around her.

As a wife, she is not having the right to express her feelings and emotions for her dead son. She is not even allowed to cry aloud and there was no one to perceive or console her. She represses her feelings and emotions. She was subservient, silent and without an existence of her own. But Sujata's sensibility leads her to a journey from a world of illusion, submission and compromise into the enlightened world of awakening and knowledge. Through her sensibility she not only understands her son's ideology but also rediscovers her own self-esteem and learns to assert it. She comes to recognize her own alienation as a wife and woman.

Sujata's process of awakening starts with Nandini, his son's beloved. She is also a victim of suffering and exploitation. Nandini had fought for the same cause. She was imprisoned and exposed to different forms of torture that left her physically and mentally drained. The policemen kept her in custody and she was subjected to extreme tortures such as sexual assault and they snatched away the vision in her eyes by putting her under the glare of thousand watt bulbs. The memory of the ignominy and humiliation that she faced in prison left a deep scar within her soul. With Sujata and Nandini, Mahasweta Devi tries to bring to light the silent sufferings and emotional imbalances of women in the society.

Mahasweta Devi's famous novel *Rudali* centres on two low-caste women, Sanichari and Bikhni, who develop a partnership for survival. They were professional mourners upon the death of upper-caste males. These women are referred to as a 'rudali' meaning 'weeping women'. Sanichari is named so because she was born on Saturday. She has been inauspicious for her own family because no one survived after her birth. She was abandoned by her mother shortly after her father's death. Bad fortune follows Sanichari even after marriage as her husband died of cholera. Her son Budhua died of tuberculosis. She lives in extreme poverty and suffering.

Continuous deaths, constant suffering and deceptions had made her into stone without any kind of emotions and feelings. Both her sensibility and sensitivity is lost because of constant suffering and misfortune. Her grief must have hardened into stone within her. After becoming a true professional mourner, she did not want to shed tears even for her near ones without paid. Sanichari had learned to adjust to her poverty and other forms of suppression. She tries to free herself from her emotional attachments and emerged out from the exploitative caste system. She got ready for her struggle of survival.

Mahasweta Devi clearly implies that women are exploited by society from all sides and in order to survive they had to take the protection of divinity, even at the cost of all other relationships or positions. Sanichari becomes a prostitute for survival. She turned out to be a powerful tool in providing moral support and empowering the marginalized women. She evolved out from a very lowly position and it is from there she attempt for and attains her emancipation.

Mahasweta Devi in her novel *The Glory of Sri Sri Ganesh* unveils the tribulation of the lower caste women in the hands of the upper caste Raiputs. She presents the sufferings of the low-caste women in Barba village, dominated by upper-caste males. The low-caste women are not allowed to many according to their wish. The Maliks decide the lives of the low-caste people. Lachima, a barber-woman, becomes the keep of Medininarayan Singh and the wet nurse of Ganesh. She is mortgaged by Gulal, her grandmother, for three bighas of land. Medininarayan keeps Lachima as he keeps bullocks and buffaloes. The upper castes do not consider the low caste as human beings; they are ill-treated, tortured and tormented. The sufferings of low-caste women are uncountable. They are abused and exploited as beasts.

Medininarayan drives away his two wives Badki and Majili for giving birth to girl child and keeps Lachima the low-caste woman for satisfying his lust. The Maliks keep low-caste women to satisfy their hot-blooded virility. In every Malik household, it is usual to keep a low-caste woman, besides the wife. The low-caste woman Lachima is not able to marry Mohar Karan whom she loved. Her sensible decision about her future husband is not possible because of being a low-caste woman. Her love feelings and emotions were hidden inside her heart. There is no one to share her feelings and she remained silent for nearly forty years.

Ganesh, the son of Medininarayan kicked his wife Putli for giving birth to a girl child. When she cried aloud in pain, he slapped her and asked her to keep quiet. A woman is not allowed to cry because the Goddess Lakshmi is being offended by such gestures. Putli is suffered from bruises on both the arms, and could not wash her hair; the head is covered with wounds by the battering of Ganesh. Rukmani is another woman a maid-servant at the house of Ganesh is being exploited by him. She is a caged bird and not even the sun or moon saw her face. She loved Kamu Ahir a low caste and wanted to marry him. But she becomes pregnant because of Ganesh and realized that she could not many Kamu Ahir, loses all interest in life, she hangs herself from the burnt out amra tree. Thus, women suffer and are silenced.

> The women did not reply. Impossible to their role in this life has not been freely chosen by them [...]. Sometimes they are landless farmers evicted from their land, sometimes kept women—these roles were decided by the higher castes. Who usually spoke while the lower castes listened. This time too the women remained silent. (28)

The upper-caste Maliks use the lower-caste women as concubines and when they become old and haggard, they are discarded and they are sent to clean the cowshed of the Maliks for food. They are not paid for their medical expenses. Women are physically and psychologically tormented and tortured by men. The misery and the historic experience of injustice dehumanise the subjects to a state of insensitivity. Thus, the lower-caste women are abused and tortured to the extreme because they were woman who is weak, submissive, gentle, and passive. They lack both the sensitivity and sensibility in their mind, body, and soul.

Thus, Mahasweta Devi's active pen brings them to life with a deep sensitivity which makes them to step out of the margins of society to live on their own. Through the characters, she pictures the real emotions and sensibility of a woman. Mahasweta Devi portrayed the women characters from a woman's point of view. Women identity is defined and inscribed within the four walls of the house. They are dependent and are not independent. In all the three novels, the women characters suffered a lot in the hands of upper-caste males. They lost all their emotions and feelings and their grief hardened into stone within them. Mahasweta Devi delineates the social predicament in which these subdued women endure all sufferings both physically and psychologically by virtue of their womanliness and sensibility.

WORKS CITED

Devi, Mahasweta. *Rudali.* Trans. Anjum Katyal. Calcutta: Seagull Books, 2010.

——. *The Glory of Sri Sri Ganesh.* Trans. Ipsita Chanda. Calcutta: Seagull Books, 2003.

——. *Mother of 1084.* Trans. Samik Bandyopadhyay. Calcutta: Seagull Books, 2011.

Ellis, Markman. *The Politics of Sensibility: Race, Gender and Commerce in the Sentimental Novel.* United Kingdom: Cambridge University Press, 1996.

Jeyashree, P.J. *Woman, a Commodity: A Reading of Mahasweta Devi's The Glory of Sri Sri Ganesh. Critical Insights into Post-Independent Indian Writing in English.* Chennai: Madras Christian College, 2012.

Kovilpillai, M. and T. Deivasigamani. "The Psychological Conflicts of Marginalized Women: A Study of Mahasweta Devi's *The Glory of Sri Sri Ganesh". Contemporary Vibes,* 8.30: 2012.

Surya, Vasantha. "Unflinching Witness." Rev. of *Rudali*: From Fiction to Performance and Five Plays. *Indian Review of Books,* 6.9.1997.

Van Sant, Ann Jessie. *Eighteenth Century Sensibility and the Novel: The Senses in Social Context.* United Kingdom: Cambridge University Press, 2004.

4

Reflection of Compromising Self of a Modern Indian Woman: 'Indu' in *Roots and Shadows*

Sandip P. Chavan

Shashi Deshpande's *Roots and Shadows*[1] explores the inner self of middle-class woman protagonist, Indu, who symbolises the 'New Women'. This is a first full-length novel of Deshpande winning Thirumati Rangammal Prize in 1984. This novel features Indu, like her counterparts in Deshpande's other novels, Sarita from *The Dark Holds No Terrors* and Jaya from *That Long Silence*, finds herself compromising and suffocating under the stranglehold of our tradition-bound society. How to reconcile woman's human demands for freedom with her need for love, nurturance and how to strike a balance between her wifehood, motherhood and career and spiritual fulfillment are some of the issues raised by the novelist in *Roots and Shadows*. In the words of P. Bhatnagar, "...the novel deals with a woman's attempt to assert her individuality and realize her freedom. It depicts how it brings her into confrontation with family, with the male world and society in general (Bhatnagar 118).

Indu, like almost each modern Indian woman, moves like a pendulum between tradition and modernity, acceptance and rejection, flexibility and rigidity, fantasy and reality, and above all, revolt and compromise. She lives with dualities and tries to find her real self but is deceived in many ways. Her journey to find her self begins from her ancestral house which she leaves to become, free and independent. In the words of Barche,

> Indu...shares the fate of Sisyphus. Her crime is the revelation of long hidden inner world of women in general and Indian

> women in particular. She is suffering in our world and her suffering is deeper and deadlier than Sisyphus's as he was to roll up only one stone, while she is rolling up many, viz., the ideal of independence and completeness, the concepts of self, sin, love, the ideal of detachment and freedom, and so on. (Barche 111)

Actually, Indu, being an educated young woman, is highly sensitive. She starts aspiring to become independent and complete in herself. She brushes aside all the age-old beliefs and superstitions prevalent in the society. As a motherless child, she was tended by the members of the joint family who never denied her any amount for care and affection. Old uncle, Kaka, Atya and other family members always cushioned her positioning in the family. But now she finds the dominant Akka, a senior member and a surrogate in the novel and the family to be a hindrance in achieving her goal of attaining independence and completeness.

Indu, from a very tender age, has always hated Akka for her narrow-mindedness. Akka doesn't allow her to meet the boy in the lone corner of the library and speaks ill of her mother. Indu rebels against the suffocating authority of Akka and the oppressive atmosphere of the family where women have no choice but to compromise submit and accept their lot. She leaves the house and later marries Jayant, a man of her own choice. But soon she realizes the futility of her search.

In her marriage with Jayant, Indu has compromised on several issues, seemingly in the belief that she was making adjustments out of love for him. She has modeled her lifestyle and her values to suit him, though he has never directly asked her to do so. She has even compromised her writing, substituting honesty with sycophantic dishonesty, just because Jayant has thought that was the order of the day. She knows that both of them are on different levels, "He chooses his level, and I...I try to choose the one he would like me to be on" (Deshpande 81). Though she is assailed by doubt, "Am I on my way to becoming an ideal woman?" (53) and knowingly sheds her 'I', and allows herself to enter passively into a relationship of submissive wife and dominating husband, deceiving herself into thinking that that is what she wants.

The novelist unfolds Indu's character and her conflict through comparison and contrast with the other women characters in the novel. One of the most important among these is Indu's cousin, Padmini (usually known and recognized as 'Mini'), whose marriage has been arranged by her parents. Although she is not actually married off in the novel, there are several indications as to the kind of man she is about to marry. The groom is neither highly educated nor good-looking. However, marriage with him does offer the prospect of security and a certain social status to Mini. The author also reveals the pragmatic aspects of arranged marriages by contrasting Mini with Indu who has both choice and freedom to shape her own life and who has also had higher education and is economically-independent. Mini, having none of these advantages, has little option but to acquiesce to the marriage, keeping in view the positive points of such an alliance. Within the social limits imposed on her, Mini emerges as a strong woman who knows what she wants and who is not swayed by sentiment. Indu, in comparison, appears confused and uncertain.

Indu too strives to seek a new environment where nobody, especially people like Akka, can exercise their wills on her. She marries Jayant, a man of different caste but of her own choice and leaves her parental home. In her very first meeting with Jayant, she is swept off her feet. He gives her a feeling of solidity and certainty. She hopes that her marriage with Jayant would enable her to realise the need to belong, to be wanted, needed and loved and, as she desired, the most primary thing for her is to win the freedom to express her true self to the world. But she painfully realizes that she has walked into just another trap, where she is forced to compromise the bitter truths of life. She does not heed the warning of Akka, who has no good opinion of inter-caste marriages, "Such marriages never work. Different castes, different languages...it's all right for a while. Then they realize..." (69).

Indu leaves her ancestral house and enters into another to be happy, independent and complete but very soon, she tastes the bitter fruits of her decision. In the words of Indu,

> Jayant and I...I wish I could say we have achieved complete happiness. But I cannot fantasise. I think of the cries that

> had filled me earlier...I want to be loved, I want to be happy. The cries are now stilled. Not because I am satisfied, or yet hopeless, but because such demands now seem to me to be an exercise in futility. Neither love nor happiness comes to us for the asking. (23)

The writer has observed that Indu's situation is a comment on how "Indian women are forced by a bigoted society to repress their sexuality"? (Mathews 8). Her marriage with Jayant suppresses her feminity and her human demands and as she begins to suppress her real feelings. She begins to experience a corresponding loss of self-esteem. She is physically and spiritually dissatisfied with her husband who takes her for granted and expects her to submit. Her love towards Jayant makes Indu to accept and compromise with what he wants and does. Her love marriage degenerates into a mere psychological affair and makes her feel that she has abused her body's sanctity. She realizes that her marriage has denied her of the fullness of experience and, therefore satisfaction or happiness. In marrying Jayant, Indu has thought that she has found, her 'alter ego', a spiritual and psychological level of closeness. She confesses,

> It was strange, the look he gave me as he went out of the room. An alter ego...isn't that a chimera we chase throughout our lives? I had thought I had found my alter ego in Jayant. I had felt that in marrying him, I had become complete.... Not only that, but total understanding. Perfect communication. And then, I had realised this was an illusion. I had felt cheated. But, can perfect understanding ever exist? (108)

But her marriage has forced her to compromise with the realization that self is an elusive centre, that one could never exchange roots with another—that this was an illusion 'a chimera' and Indu felt 'cheated'. Indu strives hard to understand the life in reality and the actual cause which is destroying her married life. But there is no perfect understanding between them, to Indu the concept of successful marriage is a hoax and she insists that nothing should be judged. She herself declares that, "Don't judge me. Don't criticise me. Just appreciate me. See only my virtues, not my vices. My strengths, not my weaknesses. This is what we want. And we call it perfect understanding" (108). She feels that her sense of certainty, confidence and assurance is being destroyed in the presence of Jayant. And when she talks of such feelings to him, he would call it only nonsense and nothing else. This becomes the crux of the problem. Jayant never bothers to understand what she really wanted, what her feelings are. To be precise, we can say that there is no real communication between them.

It is obvious that she has compromised and internalized with the patriarchal notion that a man is superior to a woman and that she is defined in his terms. Marriage to Indu appears to be only a means in procreate that's all, as she puts it,

> Behind the facade of romanticism, sentiment and tradition, what was marriage after all, but two people brought together after cold-blooded bargaining to meet, mate and reproduce so that the generations might continue? (14-15)

The tragedy of her marriage is that it fails to assure her the promised happiness. It mutilates her; it dooms her to repetition and routine, the monotony of 'meet, mate and reproduce'. Almost always it annihilates her. But a woman is not to be blamed for it. According to Simone de Beauvoir, "It is the masculine code, it is the society developed by the males and in their interest, that has established the woman's situation in a form that is at present a source of torment for both the sexes" (Beauvoir 500).

Indu searches for release from the constraints of the traditional and tradition-bound institution of marriage in search of an autonomous self, only to realize again that, "...this refuge is hard to achieve" (Deshpande 7). The paradox of the situation is that she is not completely happy with Jayant but at the same time, she cannot live without him. As Seema Suneel quotes, "Indu's marriage with Jayant denies her fullness of experience. It brings her nothing but a sense of incompleteness. It threatens to rob Indu of her self" (Suneel 65).

Ultimately, she has to compromise with the realization of the need to conform for survival and the awareness that conformity is the great destroyer of selfhood, and the only self that can be achieved is the self-born in interpersonal relationship makes Indu cry out in agony,

> This is my real sorrow. That I can never be complete in myself. Until I had met Jayant I had not known it...that there was, somewhere outside me, a part of me without which I remained incomplete. Then I met Jayant. And lost the ability to be alone. (38)

As Shivani R. Upadhyay comments, "Her idea of being complete, independent and self-contained vanishes after her marriage like dew-drops after sun-rise" (Upadhyay 48).

After a rebellious love-marriage, with Jayant, Indu slips into the conventional way of life. She attends to all the things apparently intended to please him. Before her marriage Indu ridicules Atya's idea of not saying one's husband's name as it shortens his life and of circumambulating Tulsi plant and praying for husband's life. Indu has sworn never to conform to the concept of the ideal woman as represented by her aunts and other tradition-oriented female relatives. But she realizes that with her marriage to Jayant, she has in fact compromised and conformed to the notion of the ideal woman. The conventional rituals performed by her orthodox female relatives in order to put safety and long life for their husbands are ridiculed by Indu. She remembers her confusion about it,

> What connection can there be between a man's longevity and his wife's calling him by name? It's as bad as praying to the tulsi to increase his life span. I used to watch the women piously circumambulating the tulsi, devoutly standing in front of it with folded hands and closed eyes. 'What's it for?' I had asked Atya. 'You'll understand when you get married,' she had smiled. 'What'll happen then?' 'You'll have a husband. And the tulsi...if you pray to her... she'll keep him safe. (39)

Accordingly, she is determined never to perform such self-effacing rituals that justify her existence only in relation with a man. But as per the Atya's prediction and her introspective assessment of her marriage makes her realize that, she is not different from Atya-like women as she also wishes that Jayant should be with her, always all the time, forever, and by shaping herself to suit her husband's model of a wife, she is unconsciously falling in line with the traditional women compromising and performing self-effacing rituals. Only her reasons for thinking so are different. She is also aspiring to assert her 'I'. But women like Indu are alienated from the product, upon which they work, their body, as Rosemarie Tong observes,

> A woman may say that she diets, exercises, and dresses for herself, but in reality she is probably shaping and adorning her flesh for men. A woman has little or no say about when, where, how or by whom her body will be used. (Tong 187)

It occurs to Indu that whatever she was doing, viz. looking in the mirror, dressing, undressing all, she was doing it only to please Jayant, and to please him is her survival strategy of life. It is this bitter fact of shedding her 'I', her identity in her husband's frightens Indu. After she gets married, she compromises with all the activities which her husband would like and does the same. She herself notices,

> Now I dress the way I want. As I please.... As I please? No, that's not true. When I look in the mirror, I think of Jayant. When I dress, I think of Jayant. When I undress, I think of him. Always what he wants. What he would like. What would please him. And I can't blame him. It's not he who has pressurised me into this. It's the way I want it to be. (53)

Perhaps, marriage has taught her the things like deception and artificial show. She feels that she has been deceived and made to hide her feelings. Her desire to assert herself has driven her from affection to hypocrisy. Indu realizes, "I hid my responses and emotions as if they were bits of garbage" (44).

The author has given us the glimpse of the rigid system of marriage in India which is decided not on the basis of compatibility but on caste, religion, and dowry. Indu speaks against the traditional mode of settling marriages when she sees Mini being pushed into an incompatible marriage by their elders, and accuses them, "You're leaving out that great incalculable...

human emotions" (95). But it is also true that in her own marital life also she could not free herself from, "...the shadow of submission" (145). Her reunion with Naren, a distant relation old uncle's son and her cousin, offers her an opportunity to vent her frustrations. She relates to Naren her life with Jayant in detail,

> We belong to the smart young set. Do you know what that means? ...we have to keep up with the latest trends... we don't have friends, but the right contacts and "people one should know".... And when we get together.... We talk with nostalgia of places abroad.... We discuss intelligently, even solemnly, the problems of unemployment, poverty, corruption, family planning...our hearts bleed, Naren, for Vietnam, for the blacks, for the Harijans.... But frankly, we don't care a damn...about anything but our own precious selves, our own precious walled-in lives. (33)

This emotional outburst from Indu proves that she has been exercising extreme control over herself in order to protect her marriage. It is difficult for her to accept her compromise in this matter as she has all along fooled herself that she was different from her Kakis and Atyas. As O.P. Bhatnagar comments,

> It baffled her to realize that she who had considered herself to be so independent, so intelligent, so clever; she who had been so proud of her logical and rational thinking; she who had been all set to reform Indian womanhood had fallen into the trap waiting for her. (Bhatnagar 121)

Being tied up in marriage with Jayant, Indu comes to realise that it is because of him that her life is meaningful in one view and also meaningless in another view. And she wonders why she is trying to please him all the time, in her own words, "And one day I had thought...isn't there anything I want at all? Have I become fluid, with no shape, no form of my own? At that moment a savage truth had stared me in the face.... Without wants there is no 'I'" (53).

A woman's role is not only confined to the centripetal needs of the family in which she lives but also to its centrifugal needs. It is here that a woman has to be more than her domestic role as a submissive housewife. She has to become a 'society lady', but there also, in her is a meek and yielding creature. Centuries of traditional social ethos have made her so; she compromises and takes pride in such suffering. But we do not find Indu expressing such pride in her suffering. She cannot bear with the suffering she has to face in the family and hence she breaks away from it and marries Jayant.

In the family, Indu was an incomplete being, without a sense of the wholeness of personality. But with Jayant she feels a sense of completion and wholeness, "I had felt incomplete, not as a woman, but as a person. And in Jayant, I had thought I had found the other part of my whole self" (108). But did she really attain wholeness and the integration of personality? No. She is often haunted by, "...usual feeling of total disorientation" (40). As an outsider, she remains untouched by the milieu, "For some reason I was an outsider. The waves of sorrow, sympathy and comradeship rippled all around me, but left me untouched. I did not mind. I was content to be myself" (37). Her feelings of isolation from the milieu are almost Camuesque. One is reminded here of what Meursault, an emotionally starved protagonist, says in Albert Camus' *The Outsider*, "Mother died today. Or may be yesterday. I don't know. I had a telegram from the home: 'Mother passed away. Funeral tomorrow. Yours Sincerely.' That doesn't mean anything. It may have been yesterday" (Camus 09). Such a state also reminds us of Sartre's Roquentin, who being unable to share the collective joy of the Bouvillois, stands alone saying, "But, after all, it was their Sunday, not mine..." (Sartre 81), and also feels, "...so far away...from others" (*ibid.*, 224).

This is an instance of total disorientation and isolation from which Indu too suffers. We often find in the novel references to her 'loneliness', suggested through the image of 'dust and barrenness' (20) and 'dark room' (29), which indicate that she compromises with her alienation and her disorientation finds expression when she informs us,

> Then we are out. It is dusty, a totally barren place. The glare and the heat are both fierce. I am alone now and move among people I don't know...I had rejected the family, tried to draw a magic circle around Jayant and myself. I had

> pulled in my boundaries and found myself the poorer for it. Alienation, I know now, is not the answer. On the contrary, too much of it and we can die of a terrible loneliness of the spirit. 'I am alone'...they seem to me to be the most poignant words in any language. (20-21)

In her quest for personhood and fulfilment, Indu has sought escape from family relationships but has ultimately discovered how relationships are the roots of one's being and keep on dogging one like so many shadows that make life no more substantial than a shadow; a life without identity. In fact, these roots are the shadows. Shadows that one can't flee from;

> We flatter ourselves that we've escaped the compulsions of the past; but we're still pinioned to it by little things. If not, why do I hesitate to have a cup of tea before washing and brushing? Why do I dislike the thought of a meal before I've had my bath? (41)

Even the trifles and trivial, which dog her like shadows, uproot her from her social moorings. Indu's flight from family relationships has only landed her in another trap of shadow existence waiting for her in the person of Jayant. Anguished with her confusion, she asks Naren referring to her relationship with Jayant,

> ...I've got away. But to what, Naren? To what have I got away? Is that any better than this? Is there no more to life than this? Is that any better than this? Is there no more to life than this? Are we doomed to living meaningless, futile lives? Is there no escape? (146)

Indu's decision to cut-off all family ties is a conscious choice to break out of the confining cage of subordinate womanhood. She is cognizant of the fact that her female relations have succumbed to the dictates of male authority. As a woman, Indu is hardly left with any choice. Her life is so acutely circumscribed that she cannot make quick decisions and compromises with her failure to arrive at concrete determinations,

> Inner strength...I thought of the words as I looked down on Mini's bowed head. A woman's life, they had told me, contained no choices. And all my life, especially in this house, I had seen the truth of this. The woman had no

> choice but to submit, to accept. And I had often wondered ...have they been born without wills, or have their wills atrophied through a lifetime of disuse? (17)

Indu recognizes her displacement and marginalization as a woman and a process of ego dissolution begins. She finds herself merging into others, experiencing a loss of boundaries. The authoritative and dominating male has not only suppressed the female voice for articulation but also brought silence, dullness and repulsion to the houses these women live in,

> The house was silent, as if tired of its pretence of liveliness. A few women who had been left behind, and who had been carrying on an interminable argument in the kitchen, their voices rising and falling monotonously, were now hustled out by an authoritative male voice. (17)

The author has divided Indian women, depicted in the novel, into three groups, those who follow tradition as a virtue; those who realise what is good but still are unable to come out; and those who are independent. To the first group belong the uneducated, they bank upon age-old beliefs and superstitions, and it would be hard to change them. They are foolishly sentimental and egoistic. Narmada Atya, Kaki, Sumitra Kaki, Kamala Kaki and Sunanda Atya are remarkably traditional in their manner and outlook. Akka, too, belongs to this class but without the selfishness, narrowness, powerlessness, languor, and mawkishness of any one of them. Although she has some charming qualities, yet she is not an original creation of the novelist. In the second group, none shines as brightly as Mini. Educated and to some extent aware of the peculiar situation in which she is placed, she is deeply bound by tangles of her society out of which she cannot come out with her independent voice as Indu can. She lacks willpower and too much consciousness, makes her compromise and sacrifice her self and individuality. At the other extreme stands Indu who is independent, uninhibited and the influence of the family cannot imprison her. No other character in the novel can come anywhere near her. According to M. Mini Meitei,

> The Akka family's class and caste consciousness, superstitious beliefs (such as the wife's calling of her husband by name shortens the longevity of the latter's life

> span, the eating of the husband's left over by the wife, etc.) are to Indu nothing more than putting a dead albatross around the neck of the people. (Meitei 81)

Indu, thus, is projected against the women belonging to the older generation. She differs from women who follow tradition as a virtue. She also differs from Mini who is deeply aware of her peculiar position, but makes no efforts to come out of the tangles of the society. Indu, on the other hand, rebels against the narrow conventions and particularly, the tyrannical authority of Akka on matters of education, love and marriage. She reacts, "... there was only one thing she wanted and that was to dominate" (69), and for her, it is, "A Declaration of Independence" (69). But same kind of domination is not seen in Indu's personal, married life with Jayant.

Indu's contempt for arranged marriages and for the conventional relationship shared by her Kaka and Kaki, exposes the extent of her internalization of certain stereotypical ideas. She is a 'modern' woman for whom it is fashionable to disparage all traditional relationships. Indu wonders if women like her Kaki who are devoted to their husbands are, "Martyrs, heroines, or just stupid fools?" (68). Yet, can only these three categories be applied to women who have been conditioned not to see themselves as distinct from their husband? Traditionally, this is expressed in the concept of *ardhangini*. Deshpande, throughout the novel, alerts the readers to the possibility of misjudgement on Indu's part towards these women who do not have any alternative but to enter traditionally-arranged marriages. On the other hand, there are women like Indu herself, who have the choice, but who get disappointed and surrender and compromise their freedom because of an inability to assert themselves. In spite of possessing the advantage of an educated person's understanding and exposure, Indu fails to grasp that in any relationship it is also our own responsibility to ask to be treated with dignity.

Indu broods over the fate of women in a large family and deeply resents the fact that in traditional joint Hindu families, women are nothing more than puppets, without any identity, voice or name. But her revolutionary idealism finds no takers in the family. Even Mini, according to Manjari Shukla, "...refuses to romanticise her marriage which for her is an arrangement arrived at for her own good by the elders whose wisdom must be accepted" (Shukla 99). In contrast to Indu, Mini prefers to adopt the traditional lifestyle at her ancestral home. She seeks refuge in the traditional ways of life, for there is no other way out for her. When Indu asks her about her choice of marrying, Mini's passive acceptance shocks her, as Mini says,

> What choice do I have Indu?... Millions of girls have asked this question millions of times in this country. Surely it was time they stopped asking it. What choice do I have? ...years of blind-folding can obscure your vision so that you no more see the choices.... Of course I'm marrying him because there's nothing I can do. (116-17)

Marriage, in the traditional Indian society, only means fear, agony and frustration on the girl's side. Indu learns from Mini that nothing could end except, compromise and that she has to learn to be content with her lot. Mini further states,

> Any man, Indu? Yes, any man. Any man who says "yes"... I had committed a great crime by being born a girl...I'm tired, Indu. I don't care what kind of a man he is. Once we are married, and he becomes my husband, none of his flaws will matter. (117-18)

Thus, the writer has very artistically juxtaposed different sets of women in the Indian set-up. To the old generation, represented by Akka, Narmada, Sumitra Kaki, Kamla Kaki, Sunanda Atya, a woman's life is nothing but, "To get married, to bear children, to have sons and then grand-children..." (109). And the ideal woman is the one who doesn't have her own independent identity, "A woman who sheds her personality, her real self into her husband's" (53). The other set, the new generation, represented by Indu, reviews everything with reason. Indu analyses the idea of detachment and freedom and tries to achieve these. She tries to listen to the voice of her conscience and revolts; but unfortunately has to compromise, with miserable failures in all her efforts, either due to the impact of the culture and tradition, or fear of stigma, or timidity or all these combined together.

The novelist has very exquisitely pin-pointed the inner struggles and sufferings of the new class of Indian women through the character of Indu who has raised many basic questions regarding modern women who are rooted and shaped by the Indian customs but influenced by the scientific knowledge of the West. There was a time when Indian woman was hailed as a *Pativrata*, a *Sati* and some one who has to be protected by a man. On the other hand, now she is changed person who is aware of the stirrings of her conscience, her quest, her identity, her individuality, her place and role in the family and society. Indu represents these women, and now the question before the society is whether to reject and condemn her or to encourage and cooperate with her in her efforts to establish a new image. But tragedy is that, young modern women like Indu can neither express themselves nor choose for themselves. They can neither love nor hate but compromise and be content with, "...the gift of silence" (33), that marriage has taught them. As R. Mala observes, "...these heroines are...victims of sexual paralysis" (Mala 132). Actually, they are sandwiched between tradition and modernity. Those who leave behind conviction and take the initiative to join modernity are entangled as Maria Mies observes,

> The non-conforming conduct of the women is not the consequence of an external necessity but of changed consciousness. They are not satisfied with the rhetoric of equality between man and woman, but want to see that the right to an individual life and the right to development of their individual capabilities are realized in their own lives. (Mies 29)

Indu fails to establish emotional rapport with Jayant. Indu's love-marriage degenerates into a mere psychological affair that makes her feel, "...as if there was something shameful in total commitment..." (121), and as if she has abused her body's sanctity. Indu laments for Jayant being the archetypal Indian husband, who also is shocked, "...to find passion in a woman. It puts him off. When I'm like that, he turns away from me" (82). By refusing to accept Indu's real self, her human self, Jayant forces in her a state of armed neutrality to life with him and mars the felicity of their relationship. At one stage she even contemplates leaving her husband, not because she doesn't love him but because she loves him too much and is ashamed of her love and her total dependence on her husband. She explains her frustration, her disappointment and her humiliation to Naren, the only person to whom she can open up,

> I've learnt my lesson now. And so I pretend. I'm passive. And unresponsive. I'm still and dead. And now, when you tried to kiss me, I thought...this is Jayant. So that's all I am, Naren. Not a pure woman. Not a too faithful wife. But an anachronism. A woman who loves her husband too much. Too passionately. And is ashamed of it. (82)

Consequently, Indu learns to compromise and repress her sexual desire too to maintain the status quo in her marriage. While Jayant effectively desexualizes Indu, refusing to accept her sexual personality and indirectly moulds her identity according to his prescriptions. Indu realizes that her overwhelming love for Jayant is disturbing and her total self-surrender to him is lightening. She fears that she is turning into an 'ideal' Indian wife only obeying her husband's wishes and fancies. It makes her feel like an anachronism. She hopes she can be her whole self again by being away from him and living by herself. She says, "Sometimes I wonder if I will leave him one day and live by myself. The only way in which I can be myself, my whole self again" (86).

But Indu hangs on to her marriage and beneath her passive and unquestioning submission lays her unwillingness to acknowledge her love marriage as failure. Due to the feelings of uncertainty, incompleteness and dependence, she moves between the dualities. In reality, she has failed in love, not Jayant. She has escaped from the familial responsibilities of the home, not Jayant. She realizes that marriage has stunted and hampered her individuality for she regarded it, as a 'trap' and not a bond and the home, where the family is housed, she saw it as a 'cage'. Now she realizes that all those were mere illusions and not reality and all the struggle of her life was an act of futility. Yet Jayant possesses her being. Indu tells us how good fortune for her means, "...above all. That Jayant should be with me. Always, all the time, forever..." (39), and how without him she feels, "...

cold and alone and bereft" (136). Back in her ancestral home, there is a moment of even joy but Indu wishes, "If only Jayant were here..." (38). She is therefore compelled to accept old uncle's theories, "All things are connected. Yes, they are. Which is why no one can be completely free. Freedom has to be relative" (24) and also, "Attachment.... We can't escape it. It's the law of life. You can never protect yourself against love" (102).

The novel ends with a positive note with the hope of a new dawn. The novel expounds the indelible mark carved on the psyche of women by the conventions and norms established by the society which restrict them from exhibiting their true self. The mode and style of their development inculcate in their submissiveness, silence and passiveness which has a stronghold on their psyche. Even modern, educated women consciously drape themselves with these traits and find themselves in a fix. These traits which have become the roots of femininity always cast its shadows in women's life. Deshpande seems to suggest through the present novel that a change in the upbringing of girl-child is required. Only then she would be liberated from the morals preserved for women since ages. Deshpande herself advises that,

> The world today is changing and girls are special and are valuable.... Nothing should be imposed upon her. Nothing should be marred to her. According to her potential, according to her talent she should be able to live her life. (Personal Interview Appendix I)

For a sensitive and intelligent woman like Indu—though modern, essentially Indian in sensibility—an autonomous self in a society that is largely conventional in its outlook is a myth. Her struggle to give shape and content to their individual existence in a sexist society culminates in a crisis and ends in compromise. In breaking traditional ground, she is also careful to delineate her presence on yet another dimension—as one who is qualified to defy the status quo with not only courage but also with the conviction of rationale and accountability. In a global drama involving the dance of the sexes, Indu emerges as an intelligent, attractive and wholly practical woman who is not lured into a relationship blindly but enters into it fully aware of the consequences and confident that she will be compromising with her feminine duties towards family but at the same time she is not going to stretch her moral obligations, beyond her capacity.

NOTE

1. Shashi Deshpande, *Roots and Shadows*. Chennai: Orient Longman, 2007. Print.

   (All subsequent references in the present research paper are from this edition and have been absorbed in this text by giving page references in parentheses.)

WORKS CITED

Barche, G.D. Indu Another Sisyphus in *Roots and Shadows*. *Indian Woman Novelists*. Set I, Vol. V, Ed. R.K. Dhavan. New Delhi: Prestige, 1991: 111-17.

Beauvoir, de Simone. *The Second Sex*. Picador Classics edition, London: Pan, 1988: 500.

Bhatnagar, O.P. Indian Womanhood: Fight for Freedom in *Roots and Shadows*. *Indian Women Novelists*. Set I, Vol. V, Ed. R.K. Dhavan. New Delhi: Prestige, 1991: 118-29.

Camus, Albert. *The Outsider*. Harmondsworth: Penguin, 1982: 09.

Chavan, Sandip P. *Personal Interview* (with Shashi Deshpande 30/05/2011) Appendix I. Unpublished PhD Thesis. *Compromise as a Survival Strategy in the Novels of Shashi Deshpande: A Critical Study*. SRTM University, Nanded. 2012.

Mala, R. Interview with Shashi Deshpande. *The Predicament of Indian Woman: The Heroines in the Novels of Shashi Deshpande: A Select Study*. Appendix of an Unpublished M.Phil. Dissertation. Pondicherry University: Pondicherry, July-1989: 132.

Mathews, Veena. *Demythifying Womanhood*. Deshpande talks to Mathews, *The Times of India*. Ahemadabad, 25 Sept. 1995: 8.

Meitei, M. Mini. Subverting Phallogocentrism: Feminine Discourse in *Roots and Shadows*. *The Fiction of Shashi Deshpande*. Ed. R.S. Pathak. New Delhi: Creative, 1998: 73-85.

Mies, Maria. *Indian Women and Patriarchy, Conflicts and Dilemmas of Students and Working Women*. New Delhi: Concept, 1980: 29.

Sartre, Jean Paul. *Nausea*. London: Penguin, 1965: 81.

Shukla, Manjari. *Roots and Shadows*: A Small-Scale Forsyte Saga. *The Fiction of Shashi Deshpande*. Ed. R.S. Pathak. New Delhi: Creative, 1998: 97-106.

Suneel, Seema. Shashi Deshpande, Rajendra Awasthy and Syed Abdul Malik: Life and Works. Ed. *Man-woman Relationship in Indian Fiction*. New Delhi: Prestige, 1995: 20-73.

Tong, Rosemarie. *Feminist Thought*. London: Routledge, 1993: 187.

Upadhyay, Shivani R. Deception and Dualities of Indu in *Roots and Shadows*. *Shashi Deshpande: A Critical Elucidation*. Ed. A.N. Prasad. New Delhi: Sarup, 2008: 46-55.

5

Arundhati Roy's *The Algebra of Infinite Justice*: A Work of Poetic Truth and Poetic Beauty

Amar Nath Prasad

After the success of her debut novel *The God of Small Things,* Arundhati Roy tried her best to explore some realistic picture of the society through her non-fictional works. All her critical essays which deal with the diverse themes of both the national and international upheavals are not dry and monotonous ideas, facts and statements but they are highly poetic and metaphorically integrated with the fabric of art and beauty. In her novel *The God of Small Things,* the central theme is the confrontation between the big and the small, the haves and have-nots. Similarly, her non-fictional work has also the stamp of this great gap and disparity between the high and the low. Shibu Simon says:

> Arundhati Roy, through her non-fictional writings has taken the role of a spokesperson to support the dalit and the deserted. She takes up ecology and subalternity, the major themes of her novel, as social issues in her later role as an activist. Roy makes an transition from artistic to activistic writing through her non-fictional works. The fictional subaltern characters of *The God of Small Things* are being replaced by the real subalterns in her non-fictional works. The change is from fiction to reality and from the impossible into the possible. (Simon, 10)

In her essay "The End of Imagination," Arundhati Roy has flung a very harsh and acerbic satire on the madly use of nuclear weapons for the inannihilation of the whole world and the whole community. Her language seens to be very artistic containing various poetic tools to create the human emotions on different occasions. In this essay, at one place, she seems to be very angry using so many question marks before the contemporary government and also before the contemporary social and political thinker and philosophers. Let us see one example for her passionate and angry language:

> Who the hell conducted those opinion polls? Who the hell is the Prime Minister to decide whose finger will be on the nuclear button that could turn every thing we love—our earth, our skies, our mountains, our plains, our rivers, our cities and villagers—to ash in an instant? Who the hell is he to reassure us that there will be no accidents? How does he know? Why should we trust him? What has he ever done to make us trust him? That have any of them ever done to make us trust them? (Roy, 40)

In this essay, Arundhati Roy, a great champion of the social cause and human right also casts her venom in the misuse of nuclear bomb. Like P.S. Buck, she is dead against the use of arms and ammunitions to find out a grave situation. She thinks that nuclear bomb is the men's challenge to God. She concludes the essay with a pessimistic note predicting the end of this whole earth within an hour:

> The nuclear bomb is the most anti-democratic, anti-national, anti-human, outright evil thing that man has ever made. If you are religious, then remember that this bomb is man's challenge to God. It's worded quite simply: We have the power to destroy everything that you have created. If you are not (religious) then look at this way. This world of ours is 4,600 million years old. It could end in an afternoon. (Roy, 140-41)

The second essay of this book entitled "The Greater Common Good" deals with the burning issue of the deplorable and the miserable condition of the dalit and the subalterns. In this essay, Roy acted as an activist and has tried her best to raise the voice of the voiceless affected by the Sardar Sarovar Dam in three different states of our country. These affected people, according to Roy, appealed to the State and Central Governments to listen to their views but, surprisingly enough, all their requests fell flat to them. This essay very realistically and metaphorically portrays the deplorable condition of the displaced people particularly the dalit and tribal living on the banks of Narmada river. Roy says:

> The millions of displaced people don't exist any more. When history is written they won't be in it. Not even as statistics. Some of them have subsequently been displaced three and four times—a dam, an artillery range, another dam, a uranium mine, a power project, once they start rolling there's no resting place. The great majority is eventually absorbed into slums on the periphery of our great cities where it coalesces into an immense pool of cheap construction labour (that builds more projects that displace more people). True, they are not being annihilated or takes to gas chambers, but I can warrant that the quality of their accommodation is worse than in any concentration camp of the Third Reich. They are not captive, but they redefine the meaning of liberty. (Roy, 64)

It is interesting to note that one of the important works of a writer is to expose the affectations and hollowness of men, manner, and society. In English literature, such type of writers come under the category of 'art for the sake of life'. These writers think that the society is infected with so many ills and maladies and writers are supposed to be such surgeons who are very expert in operating the wounds and other cancerous organs of society. Arundhati Roy belongs to such category of authors who exposes the reality of the society in a very satiric and literary manner. Shibu Simon and Sijo Varghese rightly say:

> The social commitment of an artist is long discussed and disputed matter in all centuries. In the 21st century, many artists consider art as a tool to help their activism. They don't take art for its own sake but for the activistic sake to bring social changes. The artists recognize the fact that activism is the need of the hour. The marginalized sections of the society face the want of support; especially the scheduled caste and the scheduled tribe. As a developing

> nation, India has to push its backward people to the main stream. (Simon, 29)

"The Greater Common Good" also brings to light India's leading problem of the storage of food grain. Roy thinks that on account of the proper facilities of storehouses, at least ten percent of the food grain is eaten by rodents and insects. So the author lays much stress on building new storehouses than building new dams for irrigation of the crops. She says:

> We must be the only country in the world that builds dams, uproots communities and submerges forests, in order to feed rats. Clearly we need better store rooms more urgently than we need dams. (Roy, 68)

The essay "The Greater Common Good" shows love and affection of Arundhati Roy to the neglected and downtrodden people. She is of the opinion that in spite of tortures and persecution, the poor people will always be silent and they'll never raise their voice against the injustice imposed by the possessed and the rich fellows of the society. She gives the terms 'the judge and the jury' to these self-centered people. She says:

> Once that's done, what do they have left? Only you. They will tern to you, because you're all they have. They will love you even while they despise you. They will trust you even though they know you well. They will vote for you even as you squeeze the very breath from their bodies. They will drink what you give them to drink. They will breath what you give them to breathe. They will live where you dump their belongings. They have to. What else can they do? There's no higher court of redress. You are their mother and their father. You are the judge and the jury. (Roy, 135)

The essay "Power Politics" has a fine fusion between feeling and form, thought and poetic sentiments. She flings harsh irony and innuendo on the self-centered mentality of the rich and the powerful to whom she gives the term "Rumpelstiltskin". This term suggests the tyranny and injustice, corruption and hypocrisy of the capitalists and materialist people who want to rule the roost everywhere and whose primary business in this life is to grease their own palms by fair means or foul. She says that Rumpelstiltskin are powerful, pitiless, and armed to the teeth. She observes:

> This realm is raw capital, his conquests emerging markets, his prayer profits, his borders, limitless, his weapons nuclear. To even try and imagine him, to hold the whole of him in your field of vision is to situate yourself at the very edge of sanity. (Roy, 46)

Arundhati Roy seems to be dead against any step concerning privatization which transfers of productive public assets from the state to private companies. All natural resources including water are productive assets given by God to the poor people. But what happens today in a country like India is the transfer of these productive public assets to the hands of the private companies. She says:

> Let's begin at the beginning. What does privatization really mean? Essentially, it is the transfer of productive public assets from the state to private companies. Productive assets include natural resources: Earth, forest, water, air. These are assets that the state holds in trust for the people. In a country like India, seventy percent of the population lives in rural areas. That's seven hundred million people. Their lives depend directly on access to natural resources. To snatch these away and sell them as stock to private companies is a process of barbaric dispossession on a scale that has no parallel in history. (Roy, 153)

This essay is also a vehement attack on the Maharashtra Electricity Board. She thinks that the poor people suffered as they had to pay exorbitant electricity bill and so many of the industrialists in Maharashtra began to generate their own power with the help of the generators. The theft of electricity is mostly done by the industrial sector:

> Who's stealing the power? Some of it no doubt is stolen by the poor—slum dwellers, people who live in unauthorized colonies on the fringes of big cities. But they donot use the heavy duty electrical gadgetry to consume the quantum of electricity we're talking about. The big stuff, the

> megawatt thievery is orchestrated by the industrial sector in connivance with politicians and government officers. (Roy, 159)

Like the previous essay "The Greater Common Good", in this essay too, once again Roy shows her deep love and sympathy to the sufferers of the Narmada Dam project. She says:

> More than half of them are Dalits, Kevats, and Kahars—ancient communities of ferrymen fisher folk, sand quarries, and cultivators of the river bed. Most of them own no land but the river sustains them and means more to them than anyone else. If the dam is built thousands of them will lose their only source of livelihood. Yet simply because they are landless they donot qualify as project affected and will not be eligible for rehabilitation.
>
> Thus, this essay presents a harsh satire on the hypocrite, the possessed and the self-centered people. Roy invites people to join in her struggle against these people. The essay ends with an optimistic and energetic calling of the author: "The boarders are open. Come on in. Let us burry Rumpelstiltskin." (Roy, 184)

It is interesting to note that Arundhati Roy strongly believes that art must have an informative and creative motto so that the ills and maladies of the society may be uprooted. About her visions and thoughts, she observes:

> I love the unanswered question, the unresolved story, the unclimbed mountain, the tender shard of an incomplete dream. Most of the time. (Roy, 197)

In her essay "The Ladies have Feelings, So...", she delineates the miserable plights of the farmers. She holds the view that the farmers are very laborious in India. Yet, they never get satisfactory amount of output due to various economic, social, and political reasons including the cold and rough attitude of the political leaders and the government machinery:

> She develops this idea of the pitiable plights of the farmers in the same essay saying that the farmers have to make a very tought competition of the mechanized corporate enterprises working thousands of acres of farmlands.

Arundhati Roy also makes the target of her harsh satire on the American President and Osama bin Laden of Afghanistan in her essay "The Algebra of Infinite Justice":

> She calls Osama 'the family secret of America', and the American President's 'dark doppelganger'. She thinks that both the President and Osama bin Laden are the enemy of humanity; "both are dangerously armed—one with the nuclear arsenal of the obscenely powerful, the other with the incandescent, destructive power of the utterly hapless. The fireball and the ice pick. The bludgeon and the axe." (Roy, 237)

The essay "War is Peace" deals with the miserable life of the people persecuted and tortured under the tyrannical attack of bombs and arsenals by America in Afghanistan. She is of the opinion that years of war has stripped these people of gentleness and made them unkind and unsympathetic towards humanity. They are so much habituated to bombs and ammunitions that for them war is a natural and routine like work and so war has become peace for them. As a result they dance to the percussive rhythms of bombs raining down around them. So, they have turned their hatred and enmity to their own people by beating, stoning and raping women, because, according to Roy, they don't seem to know what else to do with them.

Thus, this critical analysis of various essays of the book *The Algebra of Infinite Justice* by Arundhati Roy clearly shows the terror, horror, disparity and impoverishment engendered by the various man-made activities including capitalism and terrorism. But what matters most to a sensitive reader is its artistic and aesthetic presentation of the facts and figures of historical significance. Arundhati Roy, a great artist and novelist has expressed her revolutionary ideas to upgrade the position of the dalit and the deserted through artistic expressions which seem to be the core and kernel of any great piece of work of art.

WORKS CITED

Simon, Shibu and Varghese, C. *Art and Activism in Arundhati Roy,* Sarup Book Publishers Pvt. Ltd., New Delhi, 2010.

Roy, Arundhati. *The Algebra of Infinite Justice.* Penguin Books, New Delhi, 2002.

6

What is in a Name?: Naming as an Agent of Self-articulation and Mobilisation in Bharati Mukherjee's *Jasmine*

J. Samuel Kirubahar and S. Kanakaraj

Bharati Mukherjee's *Wife* presents the picture of a woman who migrates from India to America on forge papers. It also illustrates her hard encounters with men and how her name Jyoti has been changed and how she had been rechristened by the aliens she encounters in an alien soil. Jyoti takes many *avatars* and wonders at her own transformation also.

Mukherjee started writing from 1971. American dream figures predominantly in all her novels and short stories. She covers many moods of expatriation and immigration like nostalgia, frustration and hope. Mukherjee's *Jasmine* depicts the problems of the people emigrating to America with the dream of new life. As the American dream fascinates them, they undertake the hazardous journey to America. They break their social, cultural and moral obligations in a new/strange land. *Jasmine* portrays the Odyssey/exodus of the innocent village girl, *Jasmine*, through hunger, ill treatment, violence, rape and murder. Arnold Haricha Itwara in the review of *Jasmine* opines that "Named Jyoti by her grandmother and later naming herself in the vocabulary of men's changing definitions of her. Bharati Mukherjee's Jyoti-Jasmine-Jase-Jane in *Jasmine* attempts to tell a tale of pain and horror and hope in a child-woman-window's flight from debilitation in Hasnapur to 'America'" (70). *Jasmine* opens with the village astrologer under his banyan tree foretelling Jyoti's widowhood and exile. Jyoti is born in a feudal village of Punjab, eighteen years after the partition riots. The fifth daughter, and seventh of nine children of her parents, she is a dowryless, undesirable female child, a curse for them. She is bold and intelligent, the first ever likely student of Masterji fit for English education. She is a non-conformist rebel, who questions the prophecies of the astrologer about her widowhood and exile. She says to the astrologer: "you're a crazy old man. You don't know what my future hold" (3). This irritates the fortune-teller and he chucks hard on her head and she falls on the ground getting a star-shaped scar on her forehead. The scar is seen as a curse to her but she treats it as her "third eye and feels like becoming a sage"(5). She does not believe that "village girls are like cattle; whichever way you lead them, that is the way they will go" (46). In her stubbornness, she refuses to marry a widower selected by her grandmother and eventually ends up marrying Prakash Vijh in a court of law. The cursed and helpless village girl, Jyoti, becomes Jasmine, a city woman, wife of a modern man, Prakash, who wishes her "to call him by his first name" (77). She admits: "He gave me a new name: Jasmine." He said "You are small and sweet and heady one, Jasmine. You'll quicken the whole world with your perfume" (77). Prakash has a wish to secure admission in some obscure American Institute of Technology. They start dreaming about their life in America. But due to ill-luck Prakash falls a prey on the very eve of his departure rendering Jasmine heart-broken and lonely. As a born fighter and a rebel, she plans to visit the supposed institute where Prakash had to get admitted and to burn herself a 'Sati' on the campus of that engineering school. Jasmine's decision leaves her family aghast and they wonder "village girl, going alone to America without job, husband or papers?" (97). Jasmine leaves for America on forged papers knowing not what will be there in future. She muses:

> ferried in army trucks where we are roughly handled and taken to roped-off corners of waiting rooms where surely, barely wakened customs guards await their bribe. We are dressed in shreds of national customs, out of season the wilted plumage of intercontinental vagabondage. We ask only one thing to be allowed to land; to pass through; to

> continue. We sneak a look at the big departure board, the one tourists use. Our cities are there, too, our destinations are so close! But not yet, not so directly. We most sneak in, land by night in little-used strips. For us, back behind the rope in the corner of the waiting room, there is only a slate and someone who remembers to write in challan DELAYED, or TO BE ANNOUNCED, or OUT OF SERVICE. We take another of our precious dollars or Swiss francs and give it to a trustworthy-looking body and say, "Bring me tea, an Orange, bread."
>
> What country? What continent? We pass through wars, through plagues. I am hungry for news, but the discarded papers are in characters or languages I cannot read. The zigzag route is straightest. (101)

She travels to the new world on a shrimper called "The Gulf Shuttle". Her first encounter in America is what Malashri Lal in "Bharati Mukherjee: The Maximalist Credo" calls: "a regeneration through violence" (59). The captain of the ship, Half-Face, who had "lost an eye, and ear and most of his cheek in a paddy field in Vietnam" (104) takes her to a remote motel of Florida and makes her before her indecent proposals. Jasmine requests him that she is a deplorable Hindu widow and her mission is to "bring my (her) husband's suit to America. I am taking it to his school and burning it where we were going to live" (114). He laughs at it and says: "Getting your kicked half way around the world just to burn a suit. I never heard such a fool notion" (114). He remorselessly rapes her. She relates the scene: "Half-Face stood, totally naked. He was monstrously erect. Prakash had always been so concerned for me. He was afraid of youthful pregnancy, of children bearing children. He talked to me of muscles tearing, of the girl's body only looking mature, no matter what the rituals, the feudalisms, said. For the first time in my life I understood what the evil way about. It was about not being human. Half-Face was from an underworld of evil. It was a very simple, very clear perception, a moment of truth, the kind of understanding that I have heard comes at the moment of death. I had faced death twice before, and cheated it" (115-16). After her rape, she goes to the bathroom and slices her tongue and takes the *avtar* of Kali. Jasmine relates the incidents after her brutal rape by Half-Face:

> It was the murkiness of the mirror and a sudden sense of mission that stopped me. What if my mission was not yet over? I didn't feel the passionate embrace of Lord Yama that could turn a kerosene flame into a lovers caress. I could not let my personal dishonor disrupt my mission. There would be plenty of time to die; I had not yet burned my husband's suit. I had not stood under the palm trees of the college campus.
>
> I extended my tongue, and sliced it. Hot blood dripped immediately in the sink.
>
> I had planned it all so perfectly. To layout the suit, to fill it with twigs and papers. To light it then to lie upon it in the white cotton sari I had brought from home.
>
> I put on my pants and wrapped myself in the towel for the iciness outside. He was, as I had hoped, asleep in his total nakedness; hands clasped peacefully around the glass of half-drunk whiskey balanced on his chest. I drew close to the side of the bed, next to the nightstand, where I could study the good side of his face. My mouth had filled with blood. I could feel it on my chin.
>
> I began to shiver. The blade need not be long, only sharp, and my hand not strong, only quick. His eyes flutter open even before I felt the metal touch his throat, and his smile and panic were nearly instantaneous. I wanted that moment when he saw me above him as he had last seen me, naked, but now with my mouth open, pouring blood, my red tongue out. I wanted him to open his mouth and start to reach, I wanted that extra hundredth of a second when the blade bit deeper than any insect, when I jumped back as he jerked forward, slapping at his neck while blood, ribbons of bright blood, rushed between his fingers.
>
> He got his legs over the side of the bed, he stood and staggered, and with each stagger new spatter marks gushed against the walls. He kept trying to stop the blood, but the cut was small and he couldn't find where so much blood,

> his blood, was coming from. His hands kept slipping, and finally he fell of his knees at the foot of the bed. I dragged the suitcase to the farthest end of the room. He tried to rise and couldn't. I pulled the bedspread off the bed and threw it over him and then began stabbing wildly through the cloth, as the human form beneath it grew smaller and stiller. (117-19)

She remains perturbed:

> No one to call to, no one to disturb us. Just me and the man who had raped me, the man I had murdered. The room looked like a slaughter-house.
>
> Blood had congealed on my hands, my chin, my breasts. What a monstrous thing, what an infinitesimal thing, is the taking of a human life; for the second time in three months, I was in a room with a slain man, my body blooded. I was walking death. Death incarnate. (119)

And then she begins her journey, travelling light as told by Half-Face: "you crazy or what? Travel light sweetheart, always travel light" (114). Later, she happens to meet Lillian Gordon, a kind Quaker lady, who harbors her. She calls her Jazzy and teaches her to walk and talk like an American. She advises her. Jasmine ruminates:

> She forbade all discussion of it. She had a low tolerance for reminiscence, bitterness or nostalgia. Let the past make you wary, by all means. But do not let it deform you. Had I said, "I murdered a man last night," she might have said, "I'm sure you had an excellent reason. Next time, please, less salt in the eggplant." If I had said, "He raped me," she certainly would have squinted sympathetically, then said, "You're not the first and you won't be the last. Will you be needing an abortion?" She wasn't a missionary dispensing new visions and stamping out the old; she was a facilitator who made possible the lives of absolute ordinariness that we ached for. (131)

Later on, Lillian Gordon encourages Jasmine to proceed to New York for a suitable job with an introductory letter to her daughter staying there. After reaching New York, she decides to visit her husband's former teacher Davinder Vadhera, who had been instrumental in her husband's admission. His home in Flushing Queens is a part of a Punjabi immigrant ghetto. Vadhera's never come out from their four walls. Jasmine remembers her five months stay with Vadheras with pain and despair: She details:

> I felt myself deteriorating. I had gained so much weight I could't get into the cords even when I tried. I couldn't understand the soap operas. I didn't know the answers to game shows. And so I cooked, shopped, and cleaned, tended the old folks, and made conversation with Professorji when he got home.
>
> Professorji was a good man, by his lights, but he, didn't seem the same caring teacher who, in sleek blue American aerograms only months before, had tempted Prakash, his best engineering student, to leave the petty, luckless world of Jullundhar. Flushing was a neighbourhood in Jullundhar. I was spiraling into depression behind the fortress of Punjabiness. Some afternoons when Professorji was out working, and Nirmala was in her shop, and the old Vadheras were snoring through their siestas, I would find myself in the bathroom with the light off, head down on the cold, racked rim of the sink, sobbing from unnamed, unfulfilled wants. In Flushing I felt immured. An imaginary brick wall topped with barbed wire cut me off from the past and kept me from breaking into the future. I was a prisoner doing unreal time. Without a green card, even a forged one (I knew at least four men in our building who had brought themselves resident alien curds for between two and three thousand dollars), I didn't feel safe going outdoors. If I had a green card, a job, a goal, happiness would appear out of the blue. (148-49)

In the end, to the dismay, she learns that Davinder Vadhera, far from being a real professorji, is a sorter of human hair. Jasmine reveals:

> Flushing was not the downtown of dreams I'd conjured from the aerogram back in Jullundhar. And Professorji was not a professor. He was an importer and sorter of human

> hair. The hair came in great bundle from middlemen in villages as small as Hasnapur all over India. The middlemen shipped the hair in switches. Every week day Professorji sat from eight o'clock till six on a kitchen ladder-stool in a room he rented in the basement of the Khyber Bar BQ measuring and labeling the length and thickness of each separate hair.
>
> Junk hair he sold to wigmakers. Fine hair to instrument makers. Eventually, scientific instruments arid the U.S. Defense Department. It was no exaggeration to say that the security of the free world, in some small way, depended on the hair of Indian village women. His integrity as a man of science, and as a businessman, rested on the absolute guarantee that hair from Dave Vadhera met the highest standards and had been personally selected. (151-52)

Even he likes to buy Jasmine's hair. Jasmine further details the incidents:

> You could sell your hair, if you wanted to. It is eighteen inches at least, I think. We are purchasing Indian Ladies' hair only. Indian women are purists, they're cleansing their hair with berries or yogurt only, they're not ruining their hair with shampoos, gels, dyes, and permanents. American women have horrible hair—this I have learned since settling here. Their hair lacks virginity and innocence.
>
> I got the point. He needed to work here, bet he didn't have to like it. He had sealed his heart when he'd left home. His real life was in an unlivable land across oceans. He was a ghost, handing on.
>
> That's when he offered to introduce me to the master forger, another renter in the Khyber basement. He made up a fake bill of sale, my future hair when it was twenty-four inches, for three thousand dollars. He was buying my silence for his shame, and I felt the shame as well. (152-53)

After spending five frustrating months with Vadheras, one day she deserts Vadheras and sets her journey in an alien land. Jasmine then comes to meet Taylor and Wylie Hayes on Clarmont Avenue, Manhattan, as a caregiver to their adopted daughter, Duff. She discovers that Taylor is really a Professor and feels: "[...] to fall in love. I mean. I fell in love with what he represented to me, a Professor who served biscuits to a servant, smiled at her, and admitted her to the broad democracy of his joking even when she didn't understand it" (167). Taylor gives her a new name 'Jase'. In the new surroundings, Jasmine becomes more Americanized, more confident of her proficiency in English. In her early days with Duff, she takes Duff as her own child. She recalls: "Duff was my child; Taylor and Wylie were my parents, my teachers, my family" (165), but when she comes to realize that Duff is an adopted child, she wonder/muses: "I could not imagine a non-genetic child. A child that was not my own, or my husband's, struck me as a monstrous idea. Adoption was as foreign to me as the idea of widow marriage" (170). Later, she comes to realize the liquidity and transitoriness of the human relationships in America, when Wylie falls in love with an economist named Stuart Eschevman. This makes her to say:

> I realized for the first time in at least a year that America had thrown me again. There was no word I could learn, no one I could consult, to understand what Wylie was saying or why she had done it. She wasn't happy? She looked happy, sounded happy, acted happy. Then what did happy mean? Her only chance? Happiness was so narrow a door, so selective? The microwave pinged its readiness, and I started crying for my own helplessness and stupidity, but Wylie grabbed me and hugged and started crying herself, telling me it was okay, I would stay on here with Duff and Taylor; Taylor loved me and needed me, needed me even more now that there was Stuart. She said she needed me, too, and on weekends or whenever they arranged Duff's visits, I'd go to her with Duff. They weren't about to abandon me.
>
> "We love you", Wylie said, simply.
>
> I crushed my face into her sweatshirt. If I let go of her, I'd be losing everything.
>
> "Taylor loves you", Wylie said, "but you must know that."

> "Don't go", I begged. "Don't leave. Please." What was it that Taylor had explained about weak gravity? Batwinged nightmares flapped frantically; I didn't want them flying out of my skull.
>
> Two weeks later Wylie left, for Paris. She let Taylor think she might be back, might not. (181-82)

Jasmine's life in Iowa begins with her chance meeting of Ripplemeyer. She helps her getting a job in her son, Bud's, bank as a teller girl and she starts her life as a live-in-companion of Bud Ripplemeyer. But that not only gives a new life but also a new name—Jane. When Jane meets Bud, he is "a tall, fit, fifty-year-old banker, husband of Karin, father of Buddy and Vern" (14) but six months later he becomes a divorcee living within an illegal immigrant. After one year, he is a crippled man living with his Asian wife and his adopted son. Du, who is a Vietnamese brought from a refugee camp by him. Bud is always uneasy with her past and never enquires of it. Jane admits: "My genuine foreignness frightens him. I don't hold that against him. It frightens me too" (26). However, Bud courts her. She admits: "Bud courts me because I am alien. I am darkness, mystery, inscrutability. The East plugs me into instant vitality and wisdom. I rejuvenate him simply by being who I am" (200). Commenting on Jane's life with Bud, Nagendra Kumar in *The Fiction of Bharati Mukherjee: A Cultural Perspectives* says:

> Jasmine's every movement is a calculated step into her Americanization and with reach development a vital change is marked in her personality. Jasmine's flight to Iowa and her renaming as Jane is indicative of a slow but steady immersion into the mainstream American culture. Here we encounter a changed Jasmine—one who had murdered Half-Face for violating her chastity, now not only willingly embraces the company of an American without marriage but also is carrying his child in her womb. We are simply surprised at her act since every idea revolts at this form of an Indian widow. But one should never forget that she is a rebel who revolts at every step against the path drawn for her. She is an adapter, a survivor. Du is also a fighter

> who has survived eating worms and rodents in the refugee camp. Jasmine easily identifies herself with Du because both have made odysseous exploits in order to live. (115-16)

In the meantime, Du leaves her for Los Angeles to join his sister. She has started identifying herself with Du because he is also an immigrant like herself. Both of them want to become Americans. But Du's sudden departure shatters her psyche. She bursts out:

> I am amazed, and a little proud that Du had made a life for himself among the Vietnamese in Baden and I hadn't had a clue. Aside from my Dr. Jaswani and from Dr. Patel in infertility, I haven't spoken to an Indian since my month in Flushing. My transformation has been genetic; Du's was hyphenated. We were so full of wonder at how fast he became American, but he's a hybrid, like the fantasy appliances he wants to build. His high school paper did a story on him titled: 'Du (Yogi) Ripplemeyer, Vietnamese-American. (222)

So, she cries: "Suddenly I'm brawling. How dare he leave me alone out here? How dare he retreat with my admiration, my pride, my total involvement in everything he did? His education was my education. His writing and circuits were as close to Vijh & Vijh as I would ever get perhaps those two drops of soldering were my assignment in this lifetime. Now I could end it" (223). Du has been a silent companion to her. For a moment, she wants to console herself. So she thinks of Lillian Gordon who put her "on the bus that Florida morning, gave me (her) money and a kiss" (224). So she cries: "I wasn't so much to be like her. Be unsentimental, I order myself. Don't cry, don't feel sorry for yourself, be proud of what we did. He was given to us to save and to strengthen; we didn't own him, his leaving was inevitable. Even healthy" (224). Further, she consoles her thinking differently. It shows her existential concern, where being is not certain and becoming is most warranted. She realizes:

> Had things worked out differently—no Harlan Kroener, no droughts—Du would have had the father of any boy's dream, a funny,—generous, impulsive father, an American father from the heartland like the American lover I had

> for only a year. I would have had a husband, a place to call home.
>
> This, I realize, is not it.
>
> In the America, Du knows, mothers are younger than sister, mothers are illegal aliens, murderers, rape victims; in Du's America, parents are unmarried father are invalids, shot in the back on the eve of Christmas Eve.
>
> Assholes. (224)

It is because all through her life with Du she has been trying to understanding him but she fails in her attempts to real his mind as an immigrant. Hers is an anchorless option. She accepts:

> They are clues, but to what? Shadowy road signs for a phantom Columbus? I should have known about his friends, his sister, his community. I should have broken through but I was afraid to test the delicate thread of his hyphenization. Vietnamese-American: don't question either half too hard. I'm happy that he's visiting his sister. I am not grieving over the loss of a son. His sister kept him alive in the camp; we only gave him tools. From the fields, hidden in the tangles of her ratted hair, she brought him gifts of life, gifts of love: rats, roaches, crabs, snails. For every gesture of loyalty there doesn't have to be a betrayal. The star on my forehead throbs: pain and hope, hope and pain.
>
> I haven't figured out the what and why of Du's hoarding. Or maybe that's the point: exclude no option; someday your life might depend on the length of twine you squirreled away in your desk drawer. But Du's also like me, a striver and a saver, a prudent investor and money manager. I find mail-order catalogues in a language I can't read and a book of order forms. (225)

This sense of bereavement acquires intensity by the suicide of the neighbouring Lutzboy Darrel who has been in love with her though she never responds to his love. At this time, a call from Taylor sets her to move from Bud. In deserting Bud and choosing Taylor, she does not exchange between but she changes her whole world. She admits: "I am not choosing between men,

I am caught between the promise of America and old-world dutifulness. A caregiver's life is a good life, a worthy life. What am I to do? (240). When she leaves Bud, she feels:

> It isn't guilt that I feel, it's relief. I realize I have already stopped thinking of myself as Jane. Adventure, risk, transformation, the frontier is pushing indoors through uncalled windows. Watch me re-position the stars, I whisper to the astrologer who floats cross-legged above my kitchen stove.
>
> "Ready?" Taylor grins.
>
> I cry into Taylor's shoulder, cry through all the lives given birth to cry for all my dead.
>
> Then there is nothing I can do. Time will tell if I am tornado, Rubble-make, arising from nowhere and disappearing into a cloud. (240-41)

All through her stay for more than three years in Iowa with Bud, she has been faithful to him, acted like a devoted Indian wife, identified all her dreams and wishes with Bud's and sacrificed all her individuality and identity. It is a long and arduous journey, an immigrant's voyage/exodus/odyssey. Nagendra Kumar in *The Fiction of Bharati Mukherjee: A Cultural Perspective* thinks: "From the special and unique nature of her evolving 'Jasmine' self, Jane becomes, as her name implies, a non-entity, been a conscienceless 'gold digger' in Karin's words (195). From the 'Sati goddess' Jyoti (176) to the Kali—Jasmine to 'adventurous Jase' (186) to 'Plain Jane' (26) has been an eventful and uneven odyssey. The protagonist's name changes as well as her shifts in places of residence become metaphors for an immigrant woman's process of uprooting and rerooting" (118). Further, he writes: "She, however, is a complex blend of 'silent woman', the speaking person and teller of tales. As the 'silent woman' she accepts the almost preplanned and tailor-made itinerary of a certain predictable way of life with Bud. But her increasing sense of isolation and loss of self in this suffocating world is heightened by her inability to share with him her memories or reflections of the past, which are as much as part of her identity as the present" (118-19). Bud never allows her to open her past. So, he further avers: "In evaluating her past, and present and envisaging her future, she confronts the complexity and multiplicity of her identity as an immigrant woman" (119). She muses:

> I still think of myself as caregiver, recipe giver, preserver. I can honestly say all I wanted was to serve, be allowed to join, but I have created confusion and destruction wherever I go. As Karin says, I am a tornado. I hit the trailer parks first, the prefabs, the weakest links. How many more shapes are in me, how many more selves, how many more husbands? (215)

Jasmine is a good person and at the same time a blackmailer and a murderer, but she considers herself a 'love goodness' and a 'life force'. She is a 'path-finder'. She is fluid and adjusting and justifies her each and every role. It is revealed in an interview with Michael Connel where Mukherjee says: "The kinds of women I write about [...] are those who are adaptable. We've all been raised to please, been trained to be adapted wives, and that adaptability is working to the women's advantages when we come over as immigrants" (19). It is also noticed by Indira Bhatt in "Bharati Mukherjee's *Jasmine:* An Immigrant's, Attempt at Assimilation", where Bhatt avers:

> Even Jyoti to Jasmine, to Jase and Jane may appeal to be real transformation of the personality of the protagonist; from Hasnapur to Jullundhur to Florida, Manhattan, Iowa may appear to be moving from old world values to the brave new world. But the person we see, at the end of the novel moving away with Taylor, is very much the same person we encounter at the earlier stages in the novel. (177)

It is also echoed in Nagendra Kumar's *The Fiction of Bharati Mukherjee: A Cultural Perspective,* where he repeats: "In attempting to resolve her crisis of identity through nomenclature—from Jyoti to Jasmine, to Jase and to Jane—coupled with changes in geographical contours—from Hasnapur to Jullundhur, to Florida, Manhattan, Iowa—Jasmine tries all external alternatives but to no avail" (122). Gabrielle Walting in "Hybridity as Agency for the Post-Colonial Migrant: Bharati Mukherjee's *Jasmine* and Sara Suleri's *Meatless Days*" also says:

> Mukherjee has called Jasmine 'a very real feminist' who leaves behind a world despair, and has observed that the sort of gumption and/or 'husterism' she learns to show in the States evokes the image which Americans traditionally have of themselves. Thus Mukherjee suggests Jasmine is an Indian girl who makes it in America (as an Indian) than an Indian girl who becomes American. She does not make it despite her Indianness. Within days of her arrival she trades that Indianness for American walk and talk. (62)

Lillian Gordon teaches her how to become and be an American for her survival and success. Jasmine ruminates:

> Walk American, exhorted me and showed me how. I worked hard on the walk and deportment. Within a week she said I'd lost my shy sidle. She said I walked like one of those Trinidad Indian girls all thrust and cheekiness. She meant it as a compliment 'Tone it down girl!' She clapped as I took a turn between the kitchen and bath. I checked myself in the mirror, shocked at the transformation. Jazzy in a T-shirt, tight cords, and running shoes. I couldn't tell it the Hasnapur sidle I'd also abandoned my Hasnapur modesty. (132-33)

It is as C.I. Chua in "Passages from India: Migrating to America in the Fiction of V.S. Naipaul and Bharati Mukherjee" observes: "When Jasmine moves westward to a greater freedom and self-actualization, she is merely acting in the time-honoured American tradition of lighting out for the territory ahead, a territory hollowed by Horace Greeley and Twain's *Huckleberry Finn*" (59). "Jasmine embraces the subject position of the autonomous and reparcious 'New American'" (Budholia, "Hybridity" 65). T. Padma in "Diaspora, Multiple Identities and Metapsychosis: A Critique of Bharati Mukherjee's Novels" concludes: "Neither passionate but passive like Tara, nor crazed and left a shadow without feeling like Dimple, Jasmine seems to combine sentences with tenacity in making her diasporal dream a reality. Only in her case the dream seems to come true not in being in America, but becoming American something she has been yearning for the analogue in her mind (and in Bharati's) for intensity of spirit, the life-breath of willed-identity" (16).

Jasmine too has a hybrid nature. Commenting on the hybrid nature of *Jasmine*, Gabrielle Watling in "Hybridity as Agency to the Post-Colonial Migrant: Bharati Mukherjee's *Jasmine* and Sara Suleri's *Meatless Days*" observes:

> Relocation within a first world community substantially alters the post-colonial subject's experience of cultural hybridity. By definition, the post-colonial migrant is a subject who interpellates and is interpellated by a broad range of discourses, not all of which co-exist unproblematically, but western humanist expectations require that the subject consolidate his or her identity into the autonomous, unambiguous 'I' of the humanist tradition. Hybridity thus becomes shorthand for 'assimilation', a fixation of the self which requires that the migrant weed out the ambiguities born of her engagement with multiple discourses and recreate herself as 'one of us'. To put that another way the post-colonial migrant is expected to take, on western individuality and so become a 'readable' member of the First World community. Most migrants oscillate between their cultural base and the dominant First World culture, but Mukherjee's Jasmine increasingly regards the movement back and fourth between her Indian friends, family and culture and her adopted America as a sign of failure. Jasmine's early efforts to negotiate America are typical of the difficulties faced by Third World migrants in the First World, but, in adopting American values on behalf of Third World migrants, Mukherjee's work systematically overlooks the very forces which help to relegate the Asian migrant to second-class status. In short, Mukherjee's Jasmine goes beyond the adaptation which would allow her to renegotiate America on her terms and becomes a Western humanist T, a self-asserting individual for whom the voluntary negotiation of multiple discourses is anathema. (61)

Jasmine has no sentimental longing to return to her homeland. She has the spirit of the true immigrant. Brinda Bose in "A Question of Identity: Where Gender, Race and America Meet in Bharati Mukherjee" says:

> Though Jasmine comes to America with the crazy notion of erecting a funeral pyre for her dead husband's clothes on his (intended) University campus and burning herself on it, once again the notion of sanctioned suicide (Sati in this case) is rejected when America offers other possibilities. By grasping at the dream of a new life, Jasmine like the other(s) feels compelled to sacrifice most of her original self, because both the ethnicity and the womanhood that she identified with have to be massively reworked. (59)

In Mukherjee's novel, confinement becomes a major issue to women in all its perspective. It acts as a demonstration of their quest for freedom in all aspects of their lives. Dimple in *Wife* has become a prisoner of the ghetto in Flushing, Queens. Dimple, being an educated and thinking woman, is not able to accept the contradictions of her existence. She descends into repression depression, madness and murder. Her murder of her husband is an act of self-assertion and freeing of oneself/herself from the confinement. Jasmine is also confined in a similar ghetto in New York. She too cannot bear the incongruity of being a housebound young woman/widow in a city and culture. In fact, Jasmine has to face the most horrifying/grueling confrontations/experiences with death (the death of her husband, Prakash Vijh), murder (the murder of Half-Face by her after her rape by him) and suicide (the neighbor, who loved her and committed suicide when she didn't accept his proposal, Darrell). She is confined as a mother of seventeen-year-old Du (an immigrant like herself). She confines a child in her womb of a crippled man whom she leaves for the man she thinks he actually loves (Taylor). Brinda Bose in "A Question of Identity: Where Gender, Race and America Meet in Bharati Mukherjee" writes:

> In a bizarre sort of way, Jasmine is released from her traditional identity as a de-sexed widow soon after she arrives in America, for a being raped by Half-Face, murdering him, and walking out of the scene of the crime in full possession of herself, she has already transgressed all the norms she would have been expected to live by. Afterward, as she grows more confident in her powers to shape a new identity for herself, she is able to express her

> sexual desires more candidly; this culminates in her decision to reject her earlier intention of staying with the crippled Bud (whose baby she is having by artificial insemination), and to leave with Taylor, grasping at yet another change at happiness. As she asserts, she is not merely choosing between men: she is symbolically asserting her right to try and reposition the stars instead of passively accepting her fate. In America she has learned that nothing lasts forever, so she need not condemn herself to a life she does not particularly want. While freeing herself from duty, however, she does also reject the man who had renamed her Jane and had refused to acknowledge her roots; she chooses Taylor who loved her indianness, so perhaps this is an indication that having worked out the complications of a new identity, Jasmine is now ready to come to terms with her past, making the marginal the accomplice of the centre in the final analysis. (60)

Anindyo Roy in "The Aesthetics of an (Un)willing Immigrant: Bharati Mukherjee's *Days and Nights in Calcutta* and *Jasmine*" says: "As a willing immigrant, Jasmine stands poised on the American Dream, confident that she can freely refashion her life by obeying its dictates" (140). Desire for immigration to the First World can be induced in the inhabitants of the Third World through advertisements. In *Jasmine*, Jasmine is entitled by colourful brochures of American University. Commenting on Jasmine's immigrant life with Vadheras. Samir Dayal in "Creating, Preserving, Destroying: Violence in Bharati Mukherjee's *Jasmine*" affirms:

> Jasmine's temporary refuse with the Vadheras is an encounter with the insubstantiality of identity. But the Vadheras' incomparably pale ghostliness is a kind of vacuity. Mr. Vadhera is frozen in a sclerotic lie intended to cover up his humiliating and ghoulish job as a sorter of human hair; Mrs. Vadhera is caught between the simulaera of two lives. One in America and the other endlessly rehearsed on videotapes of Hindi films she watches—she dreams of both having neither. Since coming to America, Jasmine herself has felt caught between two

> different worlds, divided between near-feudalism and modernity. (76)

But Jasmine's assimilation/Americanization is not so smooth as it is observed by T. Padma in "From Acculturation to Self-Actualization: Diaspora Dream in Bharati Mukherjee's Jasmine":

> Fear, anger, pain, bitterness, confusion, silence, irony, humour as well as pathos underlines her observations as she discovers for herself the undefined median between the preservation of the old world and the assimilation into the new one. (84)

Jasmine's self undergoes an abyssal of identity. She is never at home. She is a perpetual nomad. Samir Dayal in "Creating, Preserving, Destroying: Violence in Bharati Mukherjee's *Jasmine*" is of the opinion that "The simple village girl Jyoti may have harbored the illusion of fixed identity. But as a woman—as Jasmine—she learns to resist a final or simple reversion to the assisted stereotype of the feudal Indian wife to subvert the west's desire to territorialize her, to render familiar her strangeness" (67). Commenting on Jasmine's multiple identity as an immigrant in America, Janet M. Powers also in "Sociopolitical Critique as Indices and Narrative Codes in Bharati Mukherjee's *Wife* and *Jasmine*" says:

> Bud Ripplemeyer's attraction to her is presented as a form of orientalism: to him she is exotic, mysterious and intensely sexual (*Jasmine* 200). By other men, she is mistaken for an Asian bar girl and labeled as a whore. Mary Webb expects her as an Indian to be into channeling, gurus, and out-of-body experiences. As Jane, she finds herself, a preserver, caring for a crippled man and bearing the child. In first breaking up a marriage and later deciding against a life of old world dutifulness, she takes on the identity which Bud's wife assigns her in a dream: a tornado, leaving behind a path of destruction. (103)

Jasmine's identity becomes a fluid one. She assumes many names. Hers is a divided personality. She called by different names. It results in multiple personalities. Commenting on Jasmine's identity crisis, Samir Dayal in "Creating, Preserving, Destroying: Violence in Bharati Mukherjee's *Jasmine*" says:

> Jasmine discovers identity as difference, as a multiple split subjectivity: Jyoti/Jasmine/Kali/Jase/Jane. These subjectivities and furthermore, determined by their belatedness: she does not remain simply Jyoti or anything else, but recognizes her multiplicity and ghostliness only after the violence involved in the destruction of each of the momentary condensations of self into particular named identities, each ghostly. She perpetually haunts, and is haunted by, her ghostly identities [...] Jasmine understands her own ghostliness in a more radical sense and forsakes a root identity. She recognizes within her Jasmine and cargiver but also Jase the tireless adventurer. She is thrilled by the confiding forces within herself. That is, she thrills to the contradictions and ambivalences of her own postcolonial self. She becomes a perpetual nomad and hybrid in the most radical sense; she shuffled between differing identities. (76-77)

Commenting on Jasmine's fluid identity, Pushpa N. Parekh also in "Telling Her Tale: Narrative Voice and Gender Roles in Bharati Mukherjee's *Jasmine*" says: "[...] Jasmine reacts her role as the intrepid adventurer, hurtling from the confines of an Indian widow's bleak imprisonment, she runs into the harsh brutality of illegal entry, rape, and murder in America. The ensuing silence of horror that cloaks Jasmine's world is literalized in her cutting of her tongue; Goddess Kali-like, she pours blood from her mouth on Half-Face, the moderator of evil. In Jasmine's inarticulation is exemplified her silent power to transform her self-image as Lakshmi, goodness of domestic bliss, to Kali, the war goddess" (112). Further, Parekh relates: "The voiceless Jyoti as Lakshmi and the tongueless Kali are both silent women [...]" (112). In a sense Jyoti conviction in herself as powerful and God-like is later expressed by Jasmine in terms of the goddess image Kali. Like Kali, the Jyoti Jasmine-Jane must destroy evil. Jasmine is the whole as well as single. She is all put together. Her singularity is at times revealed in various forms/acts. She exposes her love, passion, vengeance, fear and saintliness—all in one. She celebrates her singularity. Susan Koshy in "The Geography of Female Subjectivity: Ethnicity, General and Diaspora" points out that "The celebration of Jasmine's singularity is dependent on flattening out the subjectivities of the non-white women whom she encounters and identifies with, but from whom she is carefully distinguished" (69). Her singularity is expressed by the first letter in all her names. It is 'J' that announces/demonstrates her singularity. Elizabeth Bronten in "A Sense of Strangeness: The Gender and Cultural Identity in Bharati Mukherjee's *Jasmine*" comments on the 'J' in Jyoti, Jasmine, Jazzy, Jase and Jane, as follows:

> This 'J' serves as a signifier for the dialectic of a progressive engendering of identities as these bar already existing identities, putting them under erasure without consuming them. In so doing, Mukherjee's novel traces the parameters of the narrative discourse available to the muted subaltern woman. Jasmine's dislocated other speaks out of a self-conscious and self-induced effacement in the voice of a resilient, and incessantly self-refashioning hybridity. (79)

All through the novel, Jasmine, as an immigrant woman, is filled with fear, anger, pain, bitterness, confusion, silence, and pathos. She finds a median between her old world and the new one. In fact, Jasmine-Jane learns to last herself in different roles. She finds her initial identity as a silent woman in America and an invisible law-breaker. She is an illegal alien who has defied the immigration laws and a murderer. In India, she is called Jyoti, means 'light'. She carries on her forehead 'a third eye', the symbol of her arrogant refusal to be sealed by fate. As 'light', she transgresses the world of fate darkness, and death. She is renamed Jasmine by her husband. After being raped by Half-Face, she assumes the wrath of Kali and kills him in a divine frenzy. In New York, Jasmine becomes Jase. In Iowa, Jasmine is rebabtized as Jane by Bud Ripplemeyer, Jasmine's fight to Iowa and her name change to Jane indicates a slow but steady immersion into American culture. Jasmine becomes a non-entity, even a conscienceless 'gold digger' (174). She also undergoes several changes like 'Sati-goddess Jyoti', 'Kali', 'Jasmine' to 'adventurous Jase' and to 'Plain Jane'. However, Jane is a complex blend of the 'silent woman', 'the speaking person' and 'the teller of her own tale'. Commenting on Jasmine's *avatar* as Kali, Arnold Harrich Itwaru avers:

> Half-Face gave her no name. To him she was merely his prisoner, a woman-flesh-object exploited for his gratification. She killed him after he had violated her. There was no re-naming, repossessing relationship between them, no husbanding/wifing permutations. He raped her. She murdered him, and she escaped. But in the nomenclature of husbanding/wifing it is she who names herself "Kali," which is to infer that she is Kali-wife to is she who names herself "Kali," which is to infer that she is Kali-wife to this unlikely "husband". But there is a serious vilification of Kali, the Mother-Goddess of the Universe, Creator of Time and Devourer of Time, here. Kali is and can be wife to no one, nor can Kali be any mortal being. The metaphor of Kali for this woman-narrator is an exaggerated ill-conception. This divinity, Kali, like all divinities, is said to reward and to destroy, dependent on human actions in relation to the divinity's judgement. But the narrator has engaged in the erroneous stereotype which sees Kali as only a vengeful and destructive force, and in this there is a troubling romanticization of woman-power as an aggressive and destructive retaliatory force. In this manner it appears this writer shares a certain type of irresponsible populist discourse in the USA and Canada, a discourse blind to the fundamental contradictions of its own articulation. (72-73)

Such polemic discourse that one can find in romanticising and adventurising Jasmine in the form of Kali can be seen in criticism against Mukherjee's fundamental contradiction. Kali is not wife to anyone. She cannot be domesticated like Jasmine who passes from hand to hand/man to man. It is better to quote O.P. Budholia in "Dialectrics of Culture/Acculturation in Bharati Mukherjee's *Jasmine* and Anita Desai's *Journey to Ithaca*" observes that

> There comes an inner strife due to the native sensibility of *marga* as culture and the association with that culture of non-shared community in Europe. However, the pragmatic vision of Prakash is so large as the code of her inner

> psyche that she breaks the traditional bonds of society of Hasnapur for realizing the dream of Vijh and wife. She undergoes the metamorphosis of many names such as Jyoti, Jasmine, Kali, Jassy, Johane and Jane. Almost in all her names, capital /J/ occurs except /K/ in Kali. Consonant /J/ stands for *jagrukta* (awareness) of her femaleness while consonant /K/ symbolizes *kal* in the form of *Kali.* It shows that she becomes aware of the dialectics of history, culture and the cyclic movement of time. Thus, she decodes the oblique and the complicated code of history and culture. The dialectics of culture as 'sign' traces minutely the process of signifier and signified. (23-24)

The process of signifier and signified is used to multiply the complex personalities. In Jasmine, the self of a woman is segmented into polyphonic self which voices different expectations and relates to different failures. It is due to different locales on which the self of a woman is situated. All the time she is moving on from one location to the other. She loses an identity and simultaneously gains/attains a new one, even without her effort. She is poised/crucifixed. She has no choice of her own. How many multiple selves she has, she herself does not aware of them. Beena Agarwal in "Bharti Mukherjee's *Jasmine:* Breaking the Silence and Wearing the Web" points out that "Different locations assign her different roles—wife, daughter, care-taker, beloved and competent professional but at every stage she is conscious to achieve an identity of her own, along with her consciousness of her being an Indian woman. The synthesis of cultural awareness, feminist sensibility and the assertion of individuality add a new dimension to the feminist consciousness scattered in the novels of Bharati Mukherjee" (41). In fact, it can be argued that Jasmine becomes a non-entity. It is a kind of formulation of an autonomous self in an alien soil. Vijay K. Sharma in "Cross-Cultural Transactions and Evolution of Family in Bharati Mukherjee's *Jasmine*" points out that in *Jasmine* "Mukherjee celebrates the freedom of anonymous in the U.S. and the American reverence for the autonomy of the individual. The energetic protagonist of the novel, who was born as Jyoti, metamorphoses herself into personae like Jasmine, Jase, or Jane, according to the requirement of the situation" (110).

Jasmine is a female bildungsroman. It is novel which specifically traces the development of a female protagonist through various experiences and crises, into maturity, into self-identity and a place in the chaotic, modern world. Gurleen Grewal in "Born Again American: The Immigrant Consciousness in *Jasmine*" says that "The novel is an immigrant Bildungsroman and, like most narratives of Bildung, it posits a norms of self-development" (182). As Grewal indicates that the development in the novel is oriental toward making Jasmine into someone embodying the spirit of America, Mukherjee makes out six stages in Jasmine's character formation by the names she is given or given by others: the name she gets at birth is Jyoti, her husband had called her Jasmine, Little Gordon's appellation for her is Jazzy, and the Vadheras seem to have no name for her at all, Taylor calls her Jase, and Bud renames her as Jane. In all her names she undergoes a hideous process—she has to use her strength to accept all and withstand it. Commenting on Jasmine's changing identities, S. Indira in "*Jasmine*: An Odyssey of Unhousement and Enhousement" remarks: "To change from Jyoti to Jasmine, Jasmine to Jase, and Jase to Jane is not an easy process. She survived hideous times that involved rapes and murders, terrifying challenges and unimaginable crises. She is not sentimental about her Indian identity, nor does she suffer from nostalgic longing. Instead, she has used all her strength and resolve to forge new alliances in the friendly soil of the adopted homeland. The 'fusion' between the East and west pleases her and she rejoices that her journey to America has unfolded her 'affirming self'" (171). When she sets out to face the world, professorji, Lillian Gordon, Wylie and Taylor, and then Bud and Du and her family at different stages name her differently with different names. As Jasmine admits: "I have had a husband for each of the woman I've been, Prakash for Jasmine, Taylor for Jase, Bud for Jane, Half-Face for Kali" (197). She becomes a mixture of east and west, transnational and transcultural and so on. O.P. Budholia in "Dialectics of Culture and Acculturation in Bharati Mukherjee's *Jasmine* and Anita Desai's *Journey to Ithaca*" observes that the "simple girl, Jyoti, renamed Jasmine in Bharati Mukherjee's *Jasmine* reveals socio-psychological traumas relating to the life of an exile or expatriate. Based on mnemonic metaphor (gross form of memories as semantic and episodic), Jasmine works out the transoceanic, transmutationist, transnational and transcultural issues as alien native in America" (22). Further, Budholia observes: "The clash between her culture, and nature as a woman produces the concept of cross-culturalism. The cross memories (semantic(sic) and episodic) of Hasnapur becomes her national identity which comes in clash with European culture. In spite of some social and psychological differences of nationalism, the association of the two creates the third one—the composite culture of the East and the West" (24).

However, Jasmine's passage to America is characterized by a traumatic experience, the first and the worst, in a long series of adaptation, which requires her to improvise morality in order to survive. The transformation of identity from dutiful submissive widow into assertive, criminal and individualistic American woman is in full swing. From Jyoti, the village girl in Hasnapur, to Jasmine, that city woman, to Jazzy, the undocumented immigrant, to Jaze, the Manhattan nanny, to Jane, the Iowan woman, who centres the story, the 'J' will represent the element of continuity within transformation.

WORKS CITED

Agarwal, Beena. "Bharati Mukherjee's *Jasmine*: Breaking the Silence and Web." *English Literature: Voices of Indian Diaspora*. Ed. Malti Agarwal. New Delhi: Atlantic Publishers and Distributors, 2009: 40-50.

Bhatt, Indira. "Bharati Mukherjee's *Jasmine*: An Immigrant's Attempt at Assimilation." *American Literature Today*. Ed. Suman Bala. New Delhi: Prestige Books, 1994: 176-80 also in *Indian Women Novelists*. Set. III, Vol. 3. Ed. R.K. Dhawan. New Delhi: Prestige Books, 1995: 184-89 also in *The Fiction of Bharati Mukherjee: A Critical Symposium*. Ed. R.K. Dhawan. New Delhi: Prestige Books, 1996: 173-77.

Bose, Brinda. "A Question of Identity: Where Gender, Race, and America Meet in Bharati Mukherjee." *Bharati Mukherjee: Critical Perspectives*. Ed. Emmanuel S. Nelson. New York and London: Garland Publishing, 1993: 47-63.

Bronten, Elizabeth. "A Sense of Strangeness: The Gender and Cultural Identity in *Jasmine*." *Baetyl*. 2(1990): 79.

Budholia, O.P. "Dialectic of Culture/Acculturation in Bharati Mukherjee's *Jasmine* and Anita Desai's *Journey to Ithaca*." *The Quest*. Vol. 20. No. 1 (June 2006): 20-29 also in *English Literature: Voices of Indian Diaspora*. Ed. Malti Agarwal. New Delhi: Atlantic Publishers and Distributors, 2009: 27-39.

Chua, C.L. "Passage from India: Migrating to America in the Fiction of V.S. Naipaul and Bharati Mukherjee". *Reworlding—The Literature of the Indian Diaspora*. Ed. Emmanuel S. Nelson. West Port: Greenwood Press, 1992: 51-61.

Connell, Michael, Jessie Grearson and Tom Grimes. "An Interview with Bharati Mukherjee". *Iowa Review*. 20, No. 3 (Spring, 1990): 7-32.

Dayal, Samir. "Creating, Preserving, Destroying: Violence in Bharati Mukherjee's *Jasmine*". *Bharati Mukherjee: Critical Perspectives*. Ed. Emmanuel S. Nelson. New York: Carland Publishing, 1993: 65-88.

Grewal, Gurleen. "Born again American: The Immigrant Consciousness in *Jasmine*". *Bharati Mukherjee: Critical Perspectives*. Emmanuel S. Nelson. New York and London: Garland Publishing, 1993: 181-96.

Indira, S. "*Jasmine*: An Odyssey of Unhousement and Enhousement". *Commonwealth Writing: A Study in Expatriate Experience*. Eds. R.K. Dhawan and L.S.R. Krishna Sastry. New Delhi: Prestige Books, 1994: 86-90 also in *The Fiction of Bharati Mukherjee: A Critical Symposium*. Ed. R.K. Dhawan. New Delhi: Prestige Books, 1996: 169-72.

Itwaru, Arnold Harichand. "Who Jane?" *The Toronto South Asian Review*. Vol. 8, No. 2 (Winter, 1990): 70-77.

Koshy, Susan. "The Geography of Female Subjectivity: Ethnicity, Gender and Diaspora." *Diaspora*. 3.1 (1994): 69-79.

Kumar, Nagendra. *The Fiction of Bharati Mukherjee: A Cultural Perspective*. New Delhi: Atlantic Publishers, 2001.

Lal, Malashri. "Bharthi Mukherjee: 'The Maximalist' Credo". *Contemporary Indian English Fiction: Anthology of Essays*. Ed. K.N. Awasthi. New Delhi: ABS Publications 1993: 55-64.

Mukherjee, Bharati. *Jasmine*. 1989. New Delhi: Viking, 1990.

Padma, T. "Diaspora, Multiple Identities and Metampsychosis: A Critique on Bharati Mukherjee's Novels." *Indian Scholar*. Vol. 15, No. 2 (July, 1993): 1-18.

——. "From Acculturation to Self-Actualization: Diasporal Dream in Bharati Mukherjee's *Jasmine*. *Indian Women Novelists*. Set III, Vol. 3. Ed. R.K. Dhawan. New Delhi: Prestige Books 1995, 161-68.

Parekh, Pushpa N. "Telling her Tale: Narrative Voice and Gender Roles in Bharati Mukherjee's *Jasmine*". *Bharati Mukherjee: Critical Perspectives*. Ed. Emmanuel S. Nelson. New York and London: Garland Publishing Inc., 1993: 109-26.

Powers, Janet M. "Sociopolitical Critique as Indices and Narrative Codes in Bharati Mukherjee's *Wife* and *Jasmine*." *Bharati Mukherjee: Critical Perspectives*. Ed. Emmanuel S. Nelson. New York and London: Garland Publishing, 1993: 89-108.

Roy, Anindyo. "The Aesthetics of an (Un)willing Immigrant: Bharati Mukherjee's *Days and Nights in Calcutta* and *Jasmine*." *Bharati Mukherjee: Critical Perspectives*. Ed. Emmanuel S. Nelson. New York and London: Garland Publishing, 1993: 127-41.

Sharma, Vijay K. "Cross-Cultural Transactions and Evolution of Family in Bharati Mukherjee's *Jasmine*." *The Commonwealth Review*. 14.1 (Winter, 2001): 109-16.

Watling, Cabrielle. "Hybridity as Agency for the Post-Colonial Migrant: Bharati Mukherjee's *Jasmine* and Sara Suleri's *Meatless Days*." *Kunapipi*. Vol. 21, No. 1 (1999): 60-70.

7

Alienation of Women under the Perception of Feminine Sensibility in Select Novels of Bharati Mukherjee: A Study

M. Natarajan

The landscape of contemporary literature has been transformed by the rising tide of globalization in which texts are now crossing the borders of nations and cultures as newly emerging authors express their myriad voices of those once considered the subaltern. At the crest of this new literary wave is a new generation of South Asian female writers who have begun to make their unique mark upon the world of the novel.

Indian English literature originated as a necessary outcome of the introduction of English education in India under colonial rule. In recent years, it "has attracted widespread interest, both in India and abroad". It is now recognized that Indian English literature is not only part of Commonwealth literature, but also occupies a "great significance in the World literature". Today, a number of Indian writers in English have contributed substantially to modern English literature. Ram Mohan Roy who heralded the Indian Renaissance and Macaulay who recommended English language education in India were probably aware of what was in store for the Indians in terms of literary awareness. Today it "has won for itself international acclaim and distinction". Fiction, being the most powerful form of literary expression today, has acquired a prestigious position in Indian English literature. It is generally agreed that the novel is the most suitable literary form for the exploration of experiences and ideas in the context of our time, and Indian English fiction occupies its proper place in the field of literature. There are critics and commentators in England and America who appreciate Indian English novels. Prof M.K. Naik remarks:

> ...one of the most notable gifts of English education to India is prose fiction for though India was probably a fountain head of story-telling, the novel as we know today was an importation from the West. (125)

Many Indian women novelists have explored female subjectivity in order to establish an identity that is not imposed by a patriarchal society. Thus, the theme of growing up from childhood to womanhood, that is, the Bildungsroman, is a recurrent strategy. Santha Rama Rau's *Remember the House* [1956], Ruth Prawer Jhabvala's first novel *To Whom She Will* [1955] and her later *Heat and Dust* [1975] which was awarded the Booker Prize, and Kamala Markandaya's *Two Virgins* [1973] are good examples. Sex is implied in these novels, but depicted more explicitly in *Socialite Evenings* [1989] by Shobhaa De, in which she describes the exotic sex lives of the high society in Mumbai. Besides these themes, expatriate representation has been questioned on severe counts. Most expatriate writers have a weak grasp of actual conditions in contemporary India, and tend to recreate it through the lens of nostalgia, writing about 'imaginary homelands'. Distancing lends objectivity, but it can also lead to the ossification of cultural constructs, and even if memory is sharp and clear, the expatriate is not directly in contact with the reality of India.

The East/West confrontation, or the clash between tradition and modernity, is the impulse behind the works of acclaimed migrant writers, such as Meera Syal, Anita Rau Badami, Shauna Singh Baldwin, Uma Parameswaran, Chitra Banerjee Divakaruni, Anjana Appachana, and Kiran Desai. The theme of migration that leads to self-discovery, with a negation of the traditions of the country of origin, is a recurrent one among migrant authors. Bharti Kirchner's *Shiva Dancing* [1998], Ameena Meer's *Bombay Talkie* [1994] and Mukherjee, the author, to the female characters she has penned so far. Therefore, before plunging into the *mad* interstices of interpretation, a few words about the author might be of help in facilitating the understanding of the characters.

Bharati Mukherjee is an Indian-born American writer, of Bengali origins. She was born in Calcutta (now 'Kolkata'), in a well-off Brahmin family. Mukherjee's works cover several genres: novels *The Tiger's Daughter* (1971), *Wife* (1975), *Jasmine* (1981), *The Holder of the World* (1993), *Leave It To Me* (1997), *Desirable Daughters* (2002), *The Tree Bride* (2004), short-stories collections *Darkness* (1985), *The Middleman and Other Stories* (1988), *A Father,* non-fiction *The Sorrow and the Terror: The Haunting Legacy or Air India Tragedy* (1987), *Political Culture and Leadership in India* (1991), *Regionalism in Indian Perspective* (1992).

In the list of her novels and short stories *The Tiger's Daughter, Life, Jasmine, The Tree Bride, Darkness* and *The Middleman and Other Stories* are centred on female protagonists who are none but the autobiographical projection of her own self. Born in Indian society, she has been a direct witness to the restriction and atrocities inflicted upon woman in Indian patriarchy. She was well aware of limited future prospect for Indian woman as they are governed by Indian mythological values, in such a background. She could realized the problems and dilemma for the emerging class of new woman who is decked with western education and whose conscience is simultaneously formed and nourished by conservative norms and values.

Like Anita Desai, Kamala Markandaya, Shashi Deshpande, Nayantara Sahgal, Ruth Prawer Jhabvala and Githa Hariharan, Mukherjee also exposes many facets of feminism, encompassing agitation for equal opportunity, sexual autonomy and right to self-determination. Like her contemporary feminist writers she upholds the cause of women, but she differs from them because her basic concern is to delineate the problems of cross cultural conflicts faced by Indian women immigrants and how they express their sensibility. This is evident by Tara Banerjee in *The Tiger's Daughter;* Dimple in *Wife,* Jyothi in *Jasmine* and Devi in *Leave It To Me,* three sisters—Padma, Parvathi and Tara in *Desirable Daughters* and Tara in *The Tree Bride.* Bharati Mukherjee's heroines are bold an assertive. They have the strong potentiality for adaptability; they live in the firm ground of reality and accept the bitter truth of their live.

Bharati Mukherjee's female protagonists are immigrants and suffer cultural shock but they are potential women and are anxious to establish their identity by undertaking their heroic journeys. That is why she has received considerable critical attention from almost all the quarters of the globe in a relatively short period of just twenty-five years. Even though she has been acknowledged as a voice of expatriate-immigrants' sensibility, a close observation of her novels reveals that she has written all the novels with predominantly shows her views feminine sensibility. Since Bharati Mukherjee's women characters are the victims of immigration, all the critics focus her novels as problems and consequences due to immigration but actually the problems are not because they are immigrants but because the women characters fight for their rights as a woman and then as an individual how focused their sensibility.

Bharati Mukherjee has tried to create a new relationship between man and woman based on equality, non-oppression, non-exploitation so that the creative potentials of both are maximized as individuals and not gender dichotomies. The male, as a representative of the patriarchal society has, at last, being jerked off the centre of woman's gravitation. The woman is preparing now to be her own gravitational force, beyond the fullness of patriarchy. The novels of Bharati Mukherjee are based mostly on the concept of feminine sensibility. Her first novel *The Tiger's Daughter,* the protagonist Tara Banerjee returns to India after seven years stay in America. The story is drawn on Mukherjee's own experience and those of her sisters who had gone to study in America. When Tara lands at Bombay airport, she is not comfortable with her relatives. Here, Tara's Bombay relatives cannot accept a woman who not accompanied by her husband, David. According to Indian tradition, a man should lead the woman. He plays a protective role. Travelling alone, living alone and moving alone are part of unfamiliarity in many parts of India. In Indian tradition, one should marry within his caste. If anyone marries from another caste, he or she will be treated as an outcast or a sinner. But the protagonist Tara violating these rules and marries a foreign man who is a Jew. She totally forgets her caste and religion through her marriages. Ironically,

Mukherjee makes a criticism of the conservative attitude of the Indians who are crazy of foreign things and clothes but they do not appear of marriage with foreign people. In the presence of her mother, Tara feels alienated. Within herself, Tara becomes mentally turbulent and makes her return to the USA. Thus, in the first novel one could find the feeling of alienation of Tara's sensibility.

In her second novel *Wife*, the protagonist Dimple wants to break through the traditional taboos of a wife. This novel tells the story of Dimple, a seemingly docile young Bengali girl who, as any other normal girl, is full of dreams about her married life and so she eagerly and impatiently waits for marriage. She marries Amit Basu. She visualizes a new life for herself in America where Amit is expecting to immigrate. She is expected to play the role of an ideal Indian wife, stay at home and keep the house for the husband. Her frustration is built up gradually by the circumstances. She resents being wife in the Basu family and rebels against wifedom in many ways. One such way is here including a miscarriage by skipping herself free from her pregnancy, which she views as a Basu's property even in her womb. But herself-identity is avoided by marriage. She aspires for self-recognition and dream fulfillment. But Basu behaves in a different way. He wants her to a docile and submissive. So, Dimple hates Basu and his behaviour. He needs her only for sexual harassment. She feels it's a sort guilty. Finally in her mentally upset state, she kills Amit in an act of self-liberation and eventually commits suicide. The third and most accomplished novel *Jasmine* is an account of adaptation and not a defeat. It is the story of a Punjabi rural girl, Jyothi. Prakash, an energetic and enthusiastic young man enters in Jyothi's life as her husband. When Prakash prepares to go to America, she says, "I'll go with you and if you leave me, I'll jump into a well." A woman has to accept, the path of her husband, Renamed as Jasmine, joyously sharing the ambition of her husband, she looks forward going to America, a land of opportunities even this dream gets shattered by the murder of Prakash on the eve of his departure. She decides to go America and fulfill Prakash's mission and perform "Sati". Having learned to "Walk and Talk" like an American, she grabs every opportunity to become American. Jasmine becomes Jase. At the end, she kills Sukhawinder, the Khalsa lion who killed Prakash. After that she goes to Iowa assuming a new name "Jase". The manifold facets or roles played by Jasmine as Jase and Jase assault the power in woman. This power can be equal to Sakthi which is command over quality that destroys and fights against all evils. Jasmine has broken away from the shackles of caste, gender and family. She has learnt to live not for her husband or for her children but herself. Jasmine is a survivor, a fighter and an adaptor. She figures against Unfavorable circumstances, comes out a winner and carves out a new life in an alien country.

Bharati Mukherjee's succeeding novel *The Holder of the World* re-inforces expatriation as a journey of the human mind. Like Jasmine who travels westward, Hannah Estean's *Voyage to the Orient* tell us the protagonist's latest tensions, aspirations and ambitions. Hannah is born in Massachusetts who travels to India. She becomes involved with a few Indian lovers and eventually a king who gives her a diamond known as true, 'Emperor's Tear'. The story is told the detective's searching for the diamond and Hannah's viewpoint. The physical journey of the female hero not only leads to probing of the self but also makes her recognize the side of herself. She returns to her native land, not as a reformed American but a rebel living on the fringes of society. In her next novel, *Leave It To Me,* Bharati Mukherjee tells the story of a young woman sociopath named Debby Dimartino, short name Debi who seeks revenge on parents who abandoned her. The story reveals her ungrateful interaction with kind adoptive parents and a vengeful search for her real parents (described as a murderer and a flower child). The novel also looks at the conflict between Eastern and Western worlds and at mother-daughter relationships through the political and emotional involvement of the chief character in her quest for revenge.

Bharati Mukherjee's latest novel *Desirable Daughters* is a tale of immigrants and the attitude of three sisters and their ways of dealing with situations. *Desirable Daughters* as the title suggests, one kind of daughter, which parents would be proud of and for whom every parent would crave. The three sisters, who are the daughters of Motilal Bhattacharya and the great-granddaughters of Jai Krishna Gangooli, belong to a traditional Bengali Brahmin family. Padma, Parvathi and Tara are symbolic names of Shakti (Goddess of Hindu) do not flaunt the some ethical values but have the grit to carve a niche for them. They are a blend of traditional and modern outlook. Padma and Parvathi do not regret their choices, the former an immigrant of ethnic origin in New Jersey, and the latter married to a boy of her own choice and settled in the plush locality of Bombay with an encourage of servants to catch her. Tara, the narrator of the novel marries Bishwapriya Chatterjee, goes on arranged marriage. Tara finds that her married life is not fulfilling and she walks out of her traditional life, a typical American divorce settlement follows. Tara works as a volunteer in a pre-school. She enjoys her love life with Andy. Tara sends his son with his father as a divorce settlement. The fluidity of her identity, testifies not only his own but also the fluidity of the immigrants. Finally, Tara returns to her father's house for solace. This novel to a certain extent seems to be the autobiography of Bharati Mukherjee who has two sisters.

Bharati Mukherjee's last novel is *The Tree Bride*. Here the root-search links the past incidents with the present happenings of Tara's life of *Desirable Daughters*. The search to find out the identity of her stalker leads to several revelations. The plot of *The Tree Bird* moves back and forth from colonial India of the pre-independence times to San Francisco and back. Similarly, another novel *Desirable Daughters* in which the heroine Tara's venture to widen her horizons in matters of marriage, love and sex redefines her roles wife and mother.

The title of the novel *Desirable Daughters* is significant and ironical. It suggests that daughters are the object of family prestige, so their behavior should be desirable, that is to say, tune with the norms laid by the society and not abnormal. Only such daughter who do not cross the "Laxman Rekha" of etiquettes would be liked and appreciated but in the novel two daughters including the protagonist cross the borders. The three daughters of Bhattacharjee family, namely Padma, Parvati, and Tara desirable in their girlhood in the sense that they fulfill the requirement of daughterhood beauty, intelligent, obedience—and they remain confined to within four walls for the sake of family status and respect. "Our father could not let either or my sister out on the street, our car was equipped with window shades" (*DD* 29). Tara reports about her early life in Calcutta, "Our bodies changed, but our behavior did. Rebellion sounded like a lot of fun.... My life was one long childhood until I was thrown into marriage" (*DD* 27-28).

Mukherjee depicts the atrocities inflicted on 'gendered subaltern' that is, woman in the forms of child marriage, imposed arranged marriage and limited prospect of career for talented girls like Padma and Tara in the novel. Bharati Mukherjee seems to generalize the pitiable plight of woman when she comments about the tree Bird in the first chapter of the novel: "A Bengali girl's happiest night is about to become her lifetime imprisonment. It seems all the sorrows of history, all that is unfair in society and cruel in religion has settled on her" (*DD* 4). The image used for marriage indicates the oppressive confined life.

The novelist exposes her disapproval of child marriage and consequent widowhood through involvement of the story of Tree Bride Taralata. The story of Taralata who is cursed and disgraced for the death of her would-be husband and ultimately married to a tree symbolically brings out the backwardness of conservative society of India. It is totally inhuman on the part of society to deprive a girl of her inborn right to survive and fulfill her needs. The exploitation of woman in the name of religion and social prestige is denounced by the novelist. Mukherjee writes about the girl in the words, "The poor child had no idea that already she had been transferred from envied bride...into the second worst-thing in her society.... The story serves state..." (*DD* 12). The Tree Bird is symbol of self-sacrifice. The story serve as an antithesis to the life of Tara, the heroine who transgresses the boundaries laid for her. At one place, Tara says that Tree Bird has become the "model of selfless saintliness" while "my story was different, perhaps an inversion" (*DD* 280). This statement consolidates Padma's address to Tara as American, self-engrossed being. The novelist shows the contrast between the traditional woman and the modern woman: one lives for the society and sacrifice her life while the other lives a Selfish life. The Tree Bird also serves as a symbol to celebrate the liberation and independence of woman from the male domination and male support because the Tree Bird proves that a woman need not be safeguarded and supported by man: she can live even without man.

Through this novel, the novelist depicts the curses of patriarchy and different forms of exploitation upon woman. The novelist depicts marriage as the medium of exploitation rather than a desirable heavenly bliss. In Indian patriarchy, marriages are imposed on girls. Girls are not then allowed to make love marry a man of their choice especially of other cast. This issue is raised in case of Padma who established liaison with Ronald Dey, but could not marry him. "...any violation of the codes, any breath of scandal, was unthinkable" (*DD* 32). Tara's unsuccessful marriage is outcome of imposed marriage. She married a man she had never met. She married Bish because her father told her to get married. She says: "I married a man I had never met, whose picture and biography and bloodlines I approved of, because my father told me it was time to get married and this was best husband on the market" (*DD* 26).

According to the feminist Mukherjee, it is unjustified to "surrender...to the whims of fate and the manipulation of the marital marketplace.... What do they know of the needs of modern woman? (*DD* 27). Here the novelist advocates for freedom to choose one's life partner and caution us against the disasters caused by imposed marriage. We perceive irony in the failure of Tara's arranged marriage with Bish and success of love marriage of Parvati with Auro. The issue of imposed marriage upon girls is also raised in Bharati Mukherjee's other novel *Wife* in which the protagonist Dimple gets neurotic on shocking the dreams and illusions of married life and aborts her baby and kills her husband.

Tara faces the mystery of modern woman after her settlement in America. She undergoes transformation from a desirable daughter to an advanced American lady. Like the New Woman she is caught in the struggle between tradition and modernity.... As a protean heroine she braves the New World to seek her individual identity. She makes adventure in dress, food and fashion. She began to address her husband as Bishu while in India, she could not utter his name she also enjoy sexual freedom with Andy. She gives divorce to her husband because the promise of life as on American wife was not being fulfilled while knew that divorce was a shame for woman in Indian society. She wanted to drive and to work, to be economically independent. Husband in Indian conservative society is treated as god, "Sheltering tree", provider and Protector, but Tara breaks this myth and chooses another man who suit her temperament and who satisfies her sexual desires.

She rejected to be an object of sacrifice, a showpieces and a silent and submissive creature to her husband. She aspires to be loved and respected and does not want only to be provided and protected by her husband as is desired in the case of other women. So she differs from other woman. She is the protagonist of the novel because she has the unconquerable courage to excel the boundaries, to take initiation on an unknown path which may lead her to ruin. While her other sisters Padma and Parvathi had a self-righteous and passive life adopt a middle path, remain suspicious about their new identity, do not feel the need widen their horizons and are less assertive. Tara emerges as a powerful figure to meet every realizing her full potential as an independent human being. Padma lives in America, but she cling to Indian ways friend, cloths and food, Padma calls Tara "American" meaning self-engrossed. She reminds Tara to follow the models of Sita and Savitri "...things are never perfect in marriage, a woman must be prepared to accept less than perfection in this lifetime—and to model herself on Sita, Savitri and Behula, the virtuous wives of Hindu myths" (*DD* 134) but Tara chooses her own way, the instruction of Padma represent the phallocentric. The revelation of the her son's different sexual orientation leaves herself shocked for a moment, but the maturity and readiness with which she accepts the above relation speak of her modern consciousness and sensibility.

In spite of moving towards complete freedom from traditional roles, Tara cannot be separated from her roots. Her nature is Indian family norms and feels isolated and incomplete after being divorced. Presence of Bish gives her inner support which she lacks in Andy's company. She feels emptiness after separation from Bish because in her mind Bish is still her husband, 'the sheltering tree'.

The need for a husband in front of Bish shows that it is not easy for an Indian woman to be completely free from 'dependence syndromes'. She can also not avoid her motherly duties towards Rabi. Her son like Virmati of *Difficult Daughters* Tara, too, is unable to realize complete emancipation.

The novel is all about the psychological journey of the protagonist Tara from America to her cultural roots, that is India. One could visualize America and India from her perspective. The most avoided topics, that is, sex and Tara's desire for the size of organ and sexual experience with Andy, her lover and Bish have been frankly expressed. The primary issues discussed in the novel are marriage, love, sex, and dowry and woman subjugation. The three Bengali sisters represent the three different aspects of female experience. Parvati lives a complacent confined domestic life with her husband Auro, while Tara lives an ultramodern free life as a divorcee where she is provided with every opportunity to enjoy progress and liberty. Both the sister exist on two extremes whereas Padma seeks a fine balance between the two. She lives an independent life with her husband Harish Mehta and does not altogether discards her an Indian woman to follow. Padma and Parvati stick to the safer zone but Tara moves to risky and challenging role of life so she is given more importance than other two sisters.

Bharati Mukherjee's heroines are bold and assertive they have the strong potentiality for adaptability they live in the firm ground of reality and accepted the bitter truth of their life. Prof Anitha Myles opines the same when she writes that Bharati's heroines endure hardships stoically and "emerge stronger providing nourishment and stability to the entire community" in *Desirable Daughters,* all the three sisters, Padma, Parvati, and Tara break with the tradition and clichéd roles in one way. They try to adjust with the changed scenario.

Bharati Mukherjee's fiction truly reflects the temperament and mood of the present American society as experienced by immigrants in America. One of the significant themes of modern literature is the depiction of cross-cultural crisis, a subject which has assumed a great significance in the present world of globalization. Bharati Mukherjee is one of the best examples of this kind of writing or rather she is a writer from the Third World. She strongly opposed racial prejudice, and became a civil right activist. She wrote essays about the devastating effects of racism. Her mind was diverted from creative writing to matter-of-fact writing. Her writing suggests two advantages of women liberation, one, it allows them to realise their potential as individuals in the wider society, and two it is the only way by which they could achieve personal recognition and identity.

Bharati Mukherjee is not only the most commercially successful among women writers of the Indian Diaspora, but also the most controversial narrator of Indian cultural identity in a multicultural context. Like their Western counterparts, the Indian women novelists are also minutely examining the institution of marriage. The concern is higher with women writers, since marriage demands their total transformation on socio-cultural terms. The twentieth-century woman is in a state of moral dilemma Education has made her aware of her rights as an individual. The current Indian women writers like Anita Desai, Shashi Deshpande, Bharati Mukherjee and Gita Hariharan produce an interesting array of female protagonists who suffer within the framework of marriage. The twentieth century is essentially an age of unrest, doubts, and cradles of a number of complexes "isms", the sociological, psychological, and intellectual climate of the present times have undergone a thorough transformation.

To conclude, as women have experienced displacement and dislocations in personal lives, they are better suited for adaptability in an alien culture. A close reading of Mukherjee's novels reveals that her primary aim is to champion the cause of women. Mukherjee's first books weave complex tales but they lack of the art of storytelling. But her later works are more successful at capturing the readers. Thus, Bharati Mukherjee is a typical feminist writer. Her novels truly adhere to the temperament and mood of the society in which she lived.

WORKS CITED

Iyengar, K.R. Srinivasa. *Indian Writing in English*. New Delhi: Ashish Publishing House, 1993.

James, Henry. "The Art of Fiction", *American Literature of 19th Century: An Anthology*. India: Eurasia Publishing House, 1965.

Mukherjee, Bharati. *The Tiger's Daughter*. Ballantine Books (P) Ltd., New Delhi.

——. *Desirable Daughters* (New Delhi: Rupa & Co., 2004).

——. *Wife* (New Delhi: Penguin Books, 1990).

Singh, Vandana. *The Fictional World of Bharati Mukherjee*. New Delhi: Prestige Books, 1998.

Tandon, Sushma. *Bharati Mukherjee's Fiction a Perspective*. Sarup & Sons, New Delhi, 1996.

8

Portrayal of Women in Jhumpa Lahiri's *The Namesake*

R. Soundararajan and P. Murugesan

Indian women novelists have given a new dimension to Indian literature. Indian English literature has developed over a period of time and writing in English did not start in a day. It took many years and several distinguished personalities to bring the present status and distinction to Indian English literature. Indian literature is not only about novels, it is also about poetry and short stories. Before the rise of novels, several women writers composed songs, short stories and small plays. It is still believed that women are the upholders of the rich Indian tradition of fables, storytelling and more. In the mid-nineteenth century, more women started to write in English language. With the passage of time, English literature has witnessed several changes in the writing patterns. Women novelists have incorporated the recurring female experiences in their writings and it affected the cultural and language patterns of Indian literature. They have brought a stylized pattern in the whole context of Indian writing. Nowadays, people enjoy reading the Anglicized novels presented by the new age women writers.

In the 20th century, women's writing was considered as a powerful medium of modernism and feminist statements. The last two decades have witnessed phenomenal success in feminist writings of Indian English literature. Today is the generation of those women writers who have money and are mostly Western-educated. Their novels consist of the latest burning issues related with women as well as those issues that exist in the society since long. These books are thoroughly enjoyed by the masses and the publishers make easy money out of them. The publishers feel that the literature actually survives because of these types of bold topics and commercials used by the women novelists. They describe the whole world of women with simply stunning frankness. Their write-ups give a glimpse of the unexplored female psyche, which has no accessibility. The majority of these novels depict the psychological suffering of the frustrated housewife.

Indian English writing started with authors like Sarojini Naidu. This great poetess charmed the readers with her writings. Feminism themes have also been used by authors like Nayantara Sahgal and Rama Mehta. Regional fiction theme has been aptly used by Kamala Das, Anita Nair and Susan Viswanathan. Novelists like Kamala Markandaya and Anita Desai captured the spirit of Indian cultures and its traditional values. During the 1990s, India became a popular literary nation as a number of women authors made their debut in this era. Chitra Banerjee Divakaruni, Suniti Namjoshi and Anuradha Marwah Roy used realism as main theme of their novels. The list of Indian women novelists also comprises popular names such as Bharati Mukherjee, Nergis Dalal, Krishna Sobti, Dina Mehta, Indira Goswami, Malati Chendur, Gauri Deshpande, Namita Gokhale, Ruth Jhabvala, Shobhaa De, Arundhati Roy, Jhumpa Lahiri and many more. They are known for the contemporary approach in their novels. The novels of authors like Namita Gokhale or Shobhaa De are really outspoken. Most of these female novelists are known for their bold views that are reflected in their novels. Basically, these are the novels of protest and an outburst of reservations and contaminations. Unlike the past, where the works of women novelists were given less priority and were actually undervalued, classification of feministic or male writings hardly makes any sense today. Majority of the Indian readers comprising both male and female read the novels of the Indian women authors with certain expectations. They look for some "Indian-ness' in the write-ups. Only the women novelists of India are capable of conveying the messages of feminism in an Indian way.

The family saga is a tried-and-true literary genre, one that usually follows a central clan as they grow, marry, have children, age, and eventually die. There's a certain rhythm to these types of stories—unlike so many other novels, they don't focus on a particular period or event in the main characters' lives, but rather the grand, sweeping arc of a generation or sometimes generations.

People are always in the search for 'utopia' which as we all know is non-existent, the story of the better tomorrow and a happily ever after can act as the source of their strength. People migrate for better standards of living but it becomes hard task for them as the migrants leave behind everything and habituate to new and strange things. They experience a nostalgia, loss and pain of duty, a cultural and emotional vacuum in their effort to settle and adjust to the new life which are the indeed the foundations of identity.

The life of Indian communities especially that of women and the social, cultural and religious, racial and ideological conflicts faced by them in the host country becomes highly relevant here. The concept of space is very relevant in the study of communities. Cultural otherness, generational and cultural alienation from their ethnic community leaves the Indian women trapped in a space between the culture of homeland and that of the host country. They lack security and emotional support from their family and this isolation leads women who are emotionally and economically dependent on their husbands to the problems like depression, loss, and nostalgia.

Jhumpa Lahiri, an Indian by ancestry, British by birth and American by immigration is acknowledged as one of the eminent women writers in Indian English literature. Being an immigrant Lahiri is interested in the large section of new generation Indian Americans their traditions values and relationships and the significance of family and how it ties man to his homeland. Lahiri a dispassionate chronicler of the lives in a global society remains as a detached observer of the daily events in the lives of her characters. Her immigrant characters have a double vision and assert their identity in a bi-cultural universe. Her works portray the many issues that Indians settled abroad face in America.

Her novel *The Namesake* focuses on the contrasting experiences of the two generations of expatriates Ashoke and Ashima who are not inclined towards getting Americanized, while Gogol and Sonia, their children face the need to belong. The novel, the saga of Ganguli family in Culcutta and Boston portrays the struggle involved in the family, the psychological disturbance and uprooting they live with, revealing the experiences and perceptions, their hopes and aspirations traumatizing their psyche, their growing up, the circle of life and one's identity. It's a tribute to Indian women who leave their country and spent their best years of their lives in home for their children and husband. It deals with the portrayal of women in the novel especially Ashima.

Lahiri's *The Namesake,* a cross-cultural multi-generational story examines the cultural conflicts, pangs, aspirations and dilemmas of the Indian immigrants who find themselves in between the native and host cultures. *Namesake* is the story of Ashima Bhaduri, a student in degree class who becomes Ashima Ganguli after her betrothal to Ashoke Ganguli of Alipore. After marriage they shift to Boston. The book opens with Ashima Ganguly who is upset, homesick, spatially and emotionally alienated from her ancestral home, trying to recreate the taste of her favorite Indian snack, thereby trying to reconstruct her past. She thinks of her past with nostalgia of her home and spends her leisure in reading Bengali poems, stories, and articles.

Ashima's immigrant experience, identity problems, the tension between India and United States and between family tradition and individual freedom, the generation gap, the relationship between parents and children the uneasy status of the immigrants are the major themes dealt with in *The Namesake.* Ashima represents the majority of women expatriates who are reluctant to change or adapt to the culture of the host country and the social, cultural, religious, and ideological conflicts faced by them in the host country.

The first generation especially Ashima finds it very difficult to accustom to the host culture. Pregnancy was a hard time for her as there was no one to soothe her in the alien land. Motherhood is a glorious stage for a woman but for a migrant in a foreign alien land, loneliness and strange surroundings nearly kill such feelings. She was the only Indian in the hospital with three other American women in the adjoining room. Ashima "is terrified to raise a child in a country where she is related to no one, where she knows so little, where life seems so tentative and spare" (6). She is always nostalgic about her relatives in India. After Gogol's birth she says to Ashoke, "I am saying I don't want to raise Gogol alone in this country. It's not right. I want to go back" (33). Ashoke feels guilty for bringing her to this alien land. But she is determined to bear the pain and to give birth to the infant in an alien land for the sake of the child. She wants her grandmother who is staying in India to assign a name to her new born which shows her desire to hold fast to the conventions of her culture and the resulting disappointment because of the failure to do so. She suffers from sleep deprivation in a house alone with her baby and she visits the supermarket where everyone is a stranger to her. Often recalls her paralyzed grandmother and is never able to give up her Indianness. She gives her children full freedom to move out and explore the world, teaches the culture of her own country but never force them to do or practice it.

There is a perfect harmonization between Ashima and her husband. Ashima is "shattered into pieces and she feels lonely, suddenly, horribly, permanently alone" (278) after her husband's death. She decides to stay six months in States and six months in India. This move shows her new way of adaptation towards host culture. After her husband's death, she became worried about her son's marriage. Gogol marries Moushmi but her secret affair with Dimitri creates problems in their married life. Moushmi after the divorce goes to live with Dimitri and plans to leave for Paris which reveals the multi-cultural as well as the global identity of second-generation Indian immigrants. Though Ashima and Moushmi belong to the same culture, they are entirely different. For Ashima everything related to her husband is valuable but for Moushmi the things related to Gogol are just commodities carrying no importance. Ashima stand apart from all other characters in her commitment towards marriage.

Ashima is always reminded of the words of her elders who told her "not to eat beef or wear skirts or cut off her hair or forget her family" (37). But the second generation does not abide to these rules and lives a life of their own. The novel in a way portrays the problems of acculturation and assimilation faced by the first as well as the second-generation immigrants. Moushmi is a new generation Bengali born and raised in America's multicultural society and is a peculiar combination of Indian, American, and French identities. Her education at New York University, her frequent visits to France and England changed her perspectives and her native cultural consciousness. She has little appreciation for India or Indians and is more westernized in her attitude. She has privately vowed that she had never grown fully dependent on her husband (247). Their marriage relationship that developed in America's multicultural milieu ends in divorce. The second-generation immigrant Sonia when they visited Calcutta did not feel it as their home. Displacement and marginality in Sonia's case however trigger a less sense of alienation and nostalgia in her. She gradually assimilates bits and pieces of the new culture unlike Moushmi have a sense of duty and marry her boyfriend a half Chinese boy Ben. She decides to look after her mother after her father's death.

Woman in Indian English fiction is depicted as the silent sufferer and upholder of the tradition and traditional values of family and society. Born and brought up in India Ashima too upholds Indian values, traditions and culture even in America. The first-generation immigrants feel proud to their cultural past and did not like to violate their cultural past while the second generation expresses its aberrations and deviations and does not demand it or demonstrate it. Ashima as per her name "...will be without borders, without a home of her, a resident everywhere and nowhere" (276). The older immigrants are always reminded of the words of their family elders when they left India.

Ashima like many immigrant Bengali women is not culturally immunized by America's multi-culture, is a strong follower of Indian culture and gives importance to family and relationships. She does her best to perform the role of a homemaker and tries to uphold the traditional values against the materialistic values of America. The fear of losing her Bengali culture and of her children's neglect of their original culture secretly torments her.

Through the existential struggle of Ashima, Lahiri presents the pang of a woman living in an alien land, caused by a sense of isolation. She is a true representative of people whom living in similar hidden trauma. Like a traditional Indian wife in appearance and in ideologies, her life revolves around her husband and children and she sacrifices all her comforts for the sake of her family. She is true to her rule assigned to her as a daughter, granddaughter, wife and a mother and emerges as a winner.

WORKS CITED

Collu, Gabrielle. "South Asian Women Writers in North America: The Politics of Transformation", *The Literature of Indian Diaspora*. Ed. A.L. McLeod. New Delhi: Sterling, 2010.

Das, Nigamananda. *Jhumpa Lahiri Critical Perspectives*. New Delhi: Pen Craft International, 2008.

Iyengar, Shrinivasa, K.R. *Indian Writing in English*. New Delhi: Sterling, 1983.

Lahiri, Jhumpa. *The Namesake*. New Delhi: HarperCollins Publishers, 2004.

Manohar, Murali D. *Contemporary Indian Women Novelists in English*. New Delhi: Serials Publications, 2010.

Paranjape, Makarand (ed.). *In Diaspora: Theory, Histories, Texts*. New Delhi: India Log Pub. Ltd., 2001.

9

A Study on Priorities and Prerogative of Karuna in Shobhaa De's *Socialite Evenings*

R. Soundararajan and S. Chitra

Indian English fiction has always been responsive to the changes in material reality and theoretical perspectives that have impacted and governed its study since the time of its inception. At the earlier stage, the fictional works of the writers like Mulk Raj Anand, R.K. Narayan and Raja Rao were mainly concerned with the downtrodden of the society, the Indian middle-class life and the expression of traditional cultural ethos of India. At that time, even to a much later stage when writers like K.S. Venkataramani, Markandaya, Bhabani Bhattacharya, Chaman Nahal, Ruth Prawer Jhabvala, Nayantara Sahgal, Arun Joshi, and Khushwant Singh wrote Indian English fiction concentrated on the depiction of social reality of the times. And the study of these writings was largely based on realist ideology. The critical studies of their works were directed to explore how far they had been successful in giving expression to the reality around them. Much of the study was based on sociological and Marxist theoretical perspectives. Apart from the views related to the study of external reality, the psychological reality expressed through different characters formed another aspect of literary criticism.

Woman is the most adorable, meaningful and satisfying of God's creations. The extraordinary grandeur that she embodies gets fully evolved and expressed in motherhood, provided she is able to rightly conceive, understand and make use of her motherhood, not just to 'mother' her children but for the unfoldment of the 'Spiritual Truth' within her. It is then that she transforms herself into a lighthouse of wisdom, a dynamo of 'Shakti' and a harbour of solace and peace. From then onwards her contributions to the welfare of her family get reflected in society in a subtle but powerful way. She then turns into an evolutionary force of unlimited possibilities, directly or indirectly guiding the destiny of mankind. It is said that behind every successful man stands a woman—as wife or mother. Though it is one of the aspects of the perception of woman in our culture, the reality is

> The Vedas cry aloud, the Puranas shout;
> "No good may come to a woman."
> I was born with a woman's body
> How am I to attain troth?
> "They are foolish, seductive, deceptive—
> Any connection with a woman is disastrous."
> Bahina says, "If a woman's body is so harmful,
> How in the world will! reach truth?" (Bahinabai)

Woman in India, as elsewhere in the world, are facing a crisis. What exactly are they to do with themselves? They seem to be walking on a sharp-edged knife. If they are a little below the expectation of their spouse, they are dubbed as backward and useless. If they are smart and outwit their colleagues or partners in life they are looked down with suspicion and jealousy and are immediately classified as 'aggressive, unwomanly and unnatural' so where are we to draw the line? How can her gain fulfilment and satisfaction from her life and at the same time not draw unwarranted comments and criticism and also maintain her status of independence, cooperation, amiability, etc. In these days of "Identity Crisis" and women's emancipation movements, it is necessary that Indian women also discover their true identity and play their role effectively in life.

Woman has been the focus of many literary works down the centuries. In an age of development and flux in every field, one cannot easily ignore half the population. Indian writers in English have also come out of their cocoons of 'non-attachment' and have started acknowledging the status of the Indian woman in a male-dominated society. The concept of Indian womanhood is as divergent as the country itself and has undergone drastic and dramatic changes from era to era. India has travelled from her glorious past to degeneration; from spiritual ascendancy to communal clashes; from captivity to independence; from agrarian revolution to cyber technology. The role of the Indian woman has also changed from that of deity to *devadasi,* from *shakti* to *abala,* from home-bound creature to a professional.

The Indo-Anglian fiction presents a consistent picture of the changing social realities during this eventful century. Those interested in categorising may find it convenient to divide the Indian English fiction into two broad categories—the pre- and post-Independence groups of writers. The post-Independence period in the recent Indian history corresponds suitably with her concept of the 'nodal period' when a number of Indian writers of fiction in English try to explore and manifest Indian reality. In these writers, one does not find either the commitment of the earlier period or even the amused narration of the trials of the middle class, trying to unite the past traditional outlook with the fast emerging realities of the modern living conditions. In this effort, the writers of the post-Independence phase move inward. They get more and more psychologically intended and try to assess the sociological effect on the psyche of their characters.

This movement, from the outward gross realities to inward complexities, found as its mouth-piece, a number of women novelists who, by the peculiar situation of their existence, have been able to see the Indian complexities from close quarters, where constraints of varied hues and shades work upon the sensitive individuals. Fiction by women writers provides insights, a wealth of understanding, a reservoir of meanings and a basis of discussion. There has been a growing interest on women's issues and women writers focus on these issues. Many creative writings in English and many writers including Nayantara Sahgal, Shashi Deshpande and Shobhaa De have dealt with such issues.

Of the different colours and shades of the women novelists, Anita Desai is one of the many voices of the modern Indian English fiction. She is a recorder of the dilemma faced by a person in the Indian urban set up. She introduces a new age of psychological realism in this genre with her novel *Cry, The Peacock* (1963). Anita Desai, like Kamala Markandaya, has made human relationship as a centre of her fictional subject. She is mainly concerned with the journey within her characters, the main protagonists being female characters. Therefore, the repeated theme that we come across in her novels is the agony of existence in a hostile and male-dominated society which is conservative. The physical world attracts the writer to the mental apprehensions and the feeling of insecurity in the life of her protagonists who are undergoing traumatic psychic experiences due to the collapse of value-system and lack of satisfactory alternatives. Despondency, frustrations, and failures do not give rise to complete chaos and anarchy in human relationship. We see the struggle of the protagonists as heroic attempts that finally bring glory to the individual and add dignity to the spirit of freedom. As K.R.S. Iyengar has described it:

> ...the exploration of sensibility—the particular kind of Indian sensibility that is ill at ease among barbarians and the philistines, the anarchists and the amoralists. (3)

The women writers of the present century have the same thematic concerns but the treatments are their own. All of them are chroniclers of the tension in the wake of India's emergence as a developing nation. One can also find a conflict between tradition and modernity. In the novels of women writers, one comes to know about women who are traditional in their way of living but modern in their outlook and have the capacity to retain their individuality. There is a clash between awakening individuals and the dominance of the conventional social fabric where the individual finds himself/herself vulnerable.

Among the modern contemporary women novelists, Shobhaa De is a prolific Indian novelist. In 1988, she wrote her first novel *Socialite Evenings* besides she is the author of nine books, including *Strange Obsession, Sultry Day's Snapshots, Second Thoughts, Surviving Man,* and *Speed Post.*

Shobhaa De is known for her bold and frank style of writing. Feminism, its various aspects and gender equality of the society are the main themes of writing of Shobhaa De. She mainly deals with issues concerning the modern society. She also focuses on the different facets of the urban Indian society. She attempts to project the large society as a whole through her characters. Like for instance, in her novel *Socialite Evenings,* she explored the lives of the bored housewives and their loveless life of rich industrialist families. This book was critically acclaimed and it is still considered as a masterpiece. In her novel *Starry Nights,* this prominent novelist portrays the love story of two popular celluloid stars. It is the story of high-class people and it wonderfully depicts the dark side of the Hindi film industry. Shobhaa De illustrates the different characters of her books in a very beautiful and interesting way. She wonderfully presents a picture of a fragmentary world to her readers. The women characters of her novel are shown madly in love with the male characters. Love, jealousy, and manipulation are the prominent themes of Shobhaa De's books.

Shobhaa De as a writer is candid beyond our imagination. She is gifted with an extraordinary ability to discuss every sensitive aspect in her fiction. She writes very frankly about each and every aspect, of human relationship. Women sensibility in Shobhaa De's novel especially *Socialite Evenings*, she explores the lives of the wealthy urban Indians who are engaged in sexual promiscuity. It projects a new breed of women who demand equality with man in all works of life.

The lives of the "page 3" class, the agony and frustration, the tears and cattiness are ideally depicted in this marvelous novel, *Socialite Evenings.* The hollowness and emptiness of the life of the upper middleclass are ideally illustrated. *Socialite Evenings* is set at the backdrop of Mumbai high society. This is all about the lives of bored housewives of rich families whose husbands remain busy with their work and wives choose the option of extra-marital affair. Their marriages are often seen as loveless one. Their husbands are often seeing their wives as matter of respectability rather than their life partners. Karuna, the central character of this story is bored with her life with husband and now she wants to get rid of her boredom by writing a memoir. Her memoirs become successful and she achieves a lot of fame and pride in her new venture. She become a socialite and uses this prominence to get a job of advertising copywriter or a creator of a television channel. This novel was critically acclaimed but truly a masterpiece. Many women of this society can feel accustomed with the story. This story can be called as the partial autobiographical story of the author. There are some funny parts in the story when Karuna is bitchy to her friend Anjali.

She portrays modern woman Karuna in her novel *Socialite Evenings* who is aware of her 'otherness' and wants to break out. She is not submissive and compromising to the dogmas. But she grows into a different woman. Shobhaa De accounts on the oppression and exploitation of women in metropolitan cities rests on the power hierarchy in which men, the capitalists representing patriarchy, enslave cultured, educated and individualistic women. She analyses the possibility of a total independence for a woman beyond the constraints of a patriarchic society and the conditions imposed by her own biological nature. The rights of a woman to mother, or not to mother within the institution of marriage and outside marriage to about without the acceptance of a husband and to remarry or stay single are some of the hot issues to which Shobhaa De tries to find a solution through Karuna, the protagonist of this novel.

Shobhaa De elite and educated women of the upper class are entrapped in the social institution of marriage for the sake of money and honour. Marriage and family life restricts the social position of these women. As the story unfolds the life of these women, we find the sexual liberties of Anjali who at last seeks solace in religion, after her second marriage with Kumar an impotent and incompatible man; the gorgeous and vivacious Ritu who has developed flirting into a fine art and who leaves her second husband for a smuggler; Si a highly immoral character and the unhappy socialite and Karuna a prominent Bombay socialite trying to escape from the boredom of marriage and childbirth.

De's heroine Karuna belongs to a middle-class Brahmin family that tells within rigid patriarchal norms. Karuna's father an autocrat and strict always admonish his wife and three daughters. Karuna's vulnerable mother economically dependent on her male partner could say nothing against his expectations.

She couldn't prevent Karuna from getting entangled with Anjali who exposed her to the world of modeling. Karuna's mother was only a conveyor of messages from her husband to her daughter. That was how Karuna got permission to go to Delhi with Anjali for a show. Her father assertively involved his wife in all the decisions taken by him. "Your mother and I feel ashamed of all this" (*SE* 34).

The rigid nurturing of Karuna's parents had driven her close to Anjali whose liberal choice of her husband, though an unhappy marriage, had been attractive to her. Anjali too had a hateful memory of her parents strict nurturing; Karuna's yearning for the kinesthetic approach of her father is reflected in Anjali's recollection of her parent's childrearing.

> My father never did it; he was too strict and cold. I don't remember him kissing one any of us or even lightly embracing the children. (41)

It was not done to express any emotion, other than anger or disapproved. In the same way, Karuna too recalls her father's attitude. "We never sat in father's lap. In fact we rarely addressed him directly—it was always through mother" (41).

Though *Socialite Evenings* gives the readers the picture of marginalized Indian women at the hands of their husbands, De portrays the sensibility of young woman Karuna in the fascinating world of Mumbai. Karuna's marriage proves to be a total disaster. It lacks love, faith, and bonding. Karuna feels that she has married

> The wrong man for the wrong reasons at the wrong time. Her husband is 'unexciting uninspiring untutored. He was not made for introspection. (65)

However, Karuna is not afraid she faces it boldly and defiantly for she realizes, "Marriage is nothing to get excited to worry about. It is just something to get used to" (*SE* 68).

Despite her detest for her husband's callous attitude, she never feels demoralized. Rather like a "new woman" she fights back, resists, and shouts back. In a patriarchal male-dominated society, the women become marginalized and whatever is mattered to them is trivialized. Her subordination stuck her to have no choices. The Indian male in Shobhaa De novel is a person who is "terribly threatened by self-sufficient women". He is incomplete and inadequate as a husband since he lacks the traits of an ideal husband. Karuna's husband bullies, thrashes, and asserts power affirming his male chauvinism. Whereas Karuna full of facts and fantasy craves for physical desire finds reflection in her fantasies. Locked up in a fragile and futile marital knot, she has become frigid. Her pursuit finds respite in Girish in whom she finds psychological and emotional fulfillment. She wanted to be whole and without man. Woman is fragmenting a partial self. Spiritually, Karuna is spotless and unsullied.

Karuna plays different roles in different times to quench her emotional and psychic thirst. She is a model, a housewife, a society lady and an actor. She is also one of the well-known writers also.

WORKS CITED

De, Shobhaa. *Socialite Evenings.* New Delhi: Penguin Books, 1989.

Desai, Neera. *Women and Society in India.* New Delhi: Ajanta Publishers, 1969.

Devi, Usha. *Divorced Women—Socio Psychological Problems.* New Delhi: A.P.H. Publishing Corporation, 1998.

Gosh, S.K. *Women in a Changing Society.* New Delhi: Ashish Publishing House, 1984.

Raj, Pruthi and Sharma, Bela Rani. *Industrialization and Women.* New Delhi: Anmol Publications, 1995.

Srinivas Iyengar, K.R. *Indian Writings in English.* New Delhi: Sterling Publishers, 1994.

Upadhyay, H.C. *Status of Women in India.* New Delhi: Anmol Publications, 1991.

10

Romanticizing of Marriage in Manju Kapur's *A Married Woman*

Uddhav Jane

Manju Kapur is one of the rising stars in the Indian novels of the post-modern sensibility. She came into limelight with her debut *Difficult Daughters* bringing world acclaim. Today, she has five novels to her credit. Each of her novels deals in its entirety with the woman in Indian socio-political, cultural and traditional set up of society. The woman in her novels seems to have raised a war against the age-old creeds and customs prevalent in the post-modern society in a different way parallel to the Indian women novelists of the post-modern generation. She strikes a note of difference with a depiction of deviation in her women characters hitherto untraded by the feminists of Indian breed. Here in this paper it is found that the core concern of the novelist is centred around the issue of marriage pertaining to the woman's life as if a vital magical band to govern the ultimate fate of the woman even in the changed circumstances of the society. Manju Kapur gave vent to the women's suffering from intoxication of the old wine in a new bottle. Hence, her fiction attempts a critique of the romanticizing of marriage. The researcher has chosen her second novel *A Married Woman* published in 2002 to drive her point of view at home.

Marriage is an important event in the life of a woman. The importance our society attaches to marriage has found place in Indian English literature with a varying purpose. Though marriage is important both for men and women, it is observed that woman often doesn't enjoy the same freedom of thought and action as her male counterpart. In this regard, the marriage does not remain the same thing for a man as for a woman. The true position of a woman emerges if one critically probes in the rationale of the relationship of the woman with her husband. This relationship is the dominant theme of the fiction of Manju Kapur. She reflects a realistic picture of contemporary Indian woman and her relationship with her husband. She has also presented the intimate understanding of women and their problems. Her novels narrate the emergence of new sensible woman who strives to break free the shackles of patriarchal set up of family life. Manju Kapur makes them speak of love, marriage, and sex very frankly and boldly. In this regard, she is very close in the tradition of the bold writings like those of Shobhaa De, Arundhati Roy and the poetess Kamala Das. She is a highly promising writer of Indian English novel, who has acquired a permanent place in the heart of the lovers of Indian English Fiction.

Marriage, strictly speaking in a popular sense, is the relationship between man and woman, who live together as husband and wife, under sanctions from their community, religion, the current social code. Marriage acts for sexual pleasure, and for own children. In a nutshell, marriage imply continuing developmental value to man and woman and through them to the society at large, must be monogamous in nature and principle, with solid and stable bas of love; and a plinth of a morally sound character. A happy blend of love and marriage offers man and woman 'the marriage of true minds', a true fellowship—an amalgam of being and being that quickens the corporate life of two into one growing organism.

Traditions, customs, conventions, and doctrines have served their usefulness in giving it peculiar shades. The matters relating to marriage, its annulment, and the judicial separation were brought under the sole ecclesiastical jurisdiction and dealt with inhuman crudity. The Hindus disallow marriage between first cousins, which the Muslims not only freely allow, but openly encourage and, even coerce the siblings into it; and the Christians permit such a marriage only under the Episcopal Dispensation as if, that could change the nature of the relationship which is no less than the flagrant violation of the principle of the race eugenics. If a marriage, sacramental or contractual, solemnized with due rites, fails to elevate the parties above the merely physical union, is no marriage in the true meaning of the term. Woman could find no relief from marital misery, if her marriage ceased to function as a biological proposition of pleasure and progeny.

In her *A Married Woman,* Kapur brings forth those hard facts that go a long way in demystifying marriage. Astha, the only girl child of a middle-class family who's bringing up coincide the sole purpose of marriage. The novel opens with the mark of the point. "Astha was brought up properly, as befits a woman, with large supplements of fear. One slip might find her alone...unprotected" (*MW* I). Through the plight of her female protagonist, Manju Kapur has exposed that half truth, the traps, the losses, the hard realities, the anxieties, the depression, and the dangers associated with it. The experience of women and the experience of people from the basis of conflict are two divergent states. "Through the personal, private lives of these characters Manju Kapur exposes the existing tension and the oscillation of the self between the two states of mind" (Judith Stacey 51).

Manju Kapur has narrated frankly the emergence of not just an essential Indian sensibility but the depiction of cultural displacement in the culture where individualism and protest have often remained separate ideas, and the marriage and the woman's role at home is a central focus. What happens when the old customs lose their power and the woman no longer believes her life should be determined in this narrow fashion is the underlying theme and the point of concern to which Manju Kapur's *A Married Woman* invites attention on clarion call. Astha Vadera, undergoes profound changes against the backdrop of an Indian that is also evolving. There is shift in values and women have started acknowledging themselves as the co-equals of man.

As told in earlier Manju Kapur's *A Married Woman* deals with the female protagonist, Astha who is born and nurtured in a middle-class household in Delhi. Her father is a government servant and mother is a teacher in a school. Her parents are of different temperaments. Her father considers that his daughter's future lay in her own hand and also believes in the novelty. He was dissatisfied in his job and therefore he doesn't want his daughter to like himself. He encourages her to appear for the competitive exams because he thinks that a good job leads to confidence and independence. But her mother believes in the traditional ways and often declares:

> When you are married our responsibilities will be over. Do you know the Shastras say if parents die without getting their daughter married they will be condemned to perpetual rebirth? (*MW* 1)

She is always anxious about her marriage and every day in her temple in the kitchen, she prays for a good husband for Astha. She also insists Astha to pray for a worthy husband whom she follows: Astha obediently closed her eyes to delicious images of a romantic, somewhat shadowy young man holding her in his strong manly embrace (1). In spite of numerous instructions, Astha doesn't walk on the path of her parent's views. She wants to follow her own way.

From her early years, Astha is in search of true love and companionship. Astha is chained by her middle-class values at her roots. She is the only child of simple, God-fearing parents who are very protective of her and expect her moves in conformity with the tradition. "Brought up in such atmosphere, Astha's natural talent of painting takes a back-seat and her diet of 'mushy novels and thoughts of marriage' give her the wings to search for a boyfriend" (Sinha, Shalini 156).

When the day dawns, she is introduced to Bunty. His face lingers in her mind for a long.

> Day and night the thought of him kept her insides churning, she was unable to eat, sleep and study. Away from him her eyes felt dry and empty. Her ears only registered the sound of her voice. (*MW* 8)

She falls in love with him and spends too much time together planning meetings with him. Gayatri, her friend, supports her and manage everything. But unfortunately their love fails to bloom because of the obstinate traditional nature of parents. Then her young heart breaks, bleeds and wounds simultaneously. The affair makes her mother more vigilant. She forces her to marry as soon as possible: The girl is blossoming now when the fruit is ripe it has to be picked.... If she marries at this age, he will have no problem adjusting (*MW* 10).

Romantic at heart, Astha doesn't like arranged marriage. She has already taken the taste of love and considers that love alone must be the base of a lifelong relation like marriage and therefore when her mother invites a boy to see her, Astha refuses to meet him and weeps 'for the lack of love in her barren life'. The barrenness of her life is broken by Rohan, a final year student in the college. She is wholeheartedly involved with him. In the course of her action, she breaks her parent's restricted tradition and misses no opportunity to love and every moment of his company. In him she finds a sure solace from the troubles and pains of loneliness she had felt in the past. She feels transformed: Astha felt something flow inside her as she stared at his bend head. She had never been so aware of her boy's separate life before (*MW* 24).

Astha loves him so passionately that she dreams of marriage with him. Again fate mocks at her. Rohan leaves her. He goes secretly to America never again to be hers. His deception further breaks the heart of Astha and pushes her in the valley of grief: She was constantly reminded of Rohan, in the coffee house, at the back gate, at home. As for old black cars, they made her physically sick (*MW* 31).

She has changed her aim now and she decides to complete her education.

When Astha is in the final year, Hemant Wadera's family sends a proposal. Hemant is an MBA, foreign-returned son of a rich family. The boy does not believe in dowry. It makes her parents happier. On the other hand, Astha is anxious because of her former surreptitious affairs. Indian people consider that virginity is important on the wedding night and therefore girls are taught to protect their virginity as it is the gift they have to offer their husbands on the wedding night. In the patriarchy, men contempt women who are not virgin or who have been gone through in break of it by other. Really women's virginity is protected in order to ensure marriageability and determination of paternity and inheritance. These reminiscences frequently give trouble to Astha.

When Astha's M.A. exams are completed in June, her wedding is fixed. Against her romantic dreams, she is married traditionally. When all the rituals of marriage are over both the husband and wife go to Kashmir. In a houseboat in Dal Lake, the consummation take place:

> Sex. There was so much of it. The pain Astha felt between her legs was never quite absent.... Hemant attacked the whole thing with great urgency, gazing at her a little anxiously after each time, while she uncertainly smiled back to a look of satisfaction that came over his face. (*MW* 38)

Still Astha doesn't forget her lover, Rohan, and his soft and delicate kisses. But she holds Hemant in high pride for marrying her. She wants to capture her memorable moments with Hemant in words and colours:

> She tried sketching her surroundings but the beauty was too overwhelming.... She wrote a poem about the sky, the shikaras, the sound of the birds, the sum behind the mountains reflected in the water. (*MW* 39)

She is unable to find the cause of this hidden thread of chaos and unhappiness, though she is happy to find her husband looking at every sigh and sob. Hemant considers himself very fortunate to find an innocent, unspoiled, simple girl as his bride. As a motivating person, he encourages Astha for writing. Therefore, Astha feels life opening up her before in golden avenues because his words fill her heart with love. Do you think there will be golden vistas in our life, darling? (*MW* 42).

When Astha returns to Delhi, she devotes herself in the household routine of a daughter-in-law and a wife. Her sacrifice wins her the praise among the in-laws. They appreciate her and value her suggestions in family matters. Astha is artistic and imaginative in nature and she wants to enter in the profession of a journalist but her spirit is weaken when her husband considers it quite out of question, as it would require total devotion. On the other hand, a teacher's job is considered as a good time pass. Astha wonders that in the patriarchy all women were destined to be teachers or nothing. Her husband and her in-laws do not stop her from serving as a teacher in a school. Everybody thinks her job is suitable for her and everything seems fine with her in the beginning. Later her job is never considered seriously. She tries to maintain the golden mean between her job and her home. But Hemant neither respects her nor her involvement with the activities in the school.

Astha passed her early days with care, comfort and passion. Hemant becomes fully materialistic and the motto of his life is earning and hoarding more and more. He gives no time to Astha, which makes her feel alienated.

> She felt cold, dreary and distanced from him. She had been waiting for him all day, thinking of being together, but nothing of this was reciprocated. (*MW* 50)

The life and the house of Astha turn into the hell of exploitation from heaven of happiness. Their relation becomes merely the means of sexuality. Hemant doesn't provide her needed companionship and emotional attachment. He expresses his indifference and annoyance even on trivial matters. As a simple middle-class girl, she has very few material needs. She deeply believes in the values of love and possessiveness within the family. She gradually knows that there is a big difference between her and her corporate husband. Hemant pays more attention towards his progress than to look after his wife. This emotional incompatibility leads her to angst and depression.

Hemant is unhappy with the idea of Astha that she wants to stay her mother with her when Astha's father dies. Whenever she appeals, it irritated and annoyed him. Her helpless and uncared mother finds shelter in a Swami's Ashram. Astha feels hurt and discriminated and therefore she gets distracted from her husband. She gets further shock sensing Hemant's reluctance to see her become a mother.

Astha feels and receives comfort to observe his caring attitude all through her pregnancy:

> He loved touching her belly and breasts, her breasts especially, sucking on them experimentally, drawing a little milk when he sucked long enough. (*MW* 58)

Her dream is satisfied with the birth of a girl child, and because of the child she feels like a complete woman. He is also proud to be a father but he is more inclined to a son than to a daughter. Even the pan-American husband couldn't abstain from desiring a son and her heir: "I was so pleased Anu was a girl. But that doesn't mean we should not try for a boy...we will have a son, and if we don't we needn't stop at two" (*MW* 61). Astha becomes pregnant second time, and this time everybody in the family expects a boy: "All had an opinion about her baby's gender, and that almost universal opinion was that it would be a son and heir" (69).

Astha satisfies the expectations of the family when she gives birth to a son. Even Astha's mother overwhelmingly becomes happy because of the birth of her grandson, the carrier of the line, the seed, and the name.

Astha hates the gender prejudice in the family. She is surprised to see the family to celebrate the birth of a boy. The boy's birth is celebrated ceremoniously by giving gold jewelry and a new sari to Astha. Anuradha's birth, on the other hand, could draw only a light response and celebration. Astha feels pride of her status of motherhood and Hemant's felicity flows through her like a river: "Astha often looked at her family, husband, daughter and son. She had them all. She was fulfilled" (60). She considers that she has become the archetypal model of the female race and female experiences. But she dislikes the superstitious belief regarding a male and female child.

Now everything is going well in the family. Hemant makes very good progress in his business. He goes on the tours of foreign frequently. The prosperity however proves a cause of great trouble to Astha. She feels lonely and alienated in the family. She gives top priority to job because she wants to become independent and Hemant too expect that she should bear all her expenses.

Though everything is in proper tune, Astha's miseries follow her. The proper nourishment of kids, looking after husband and family and anxiety about job scenario had bad effects on Astha's health and she starts having headaches and sickness with wrinkled eye-brows and drawn face. In this condition of ill health, Hemant gives no attention towards her, i.e. he becomes an inattentive and absent husband. She doesn't pay heed towards her job because of the responsibilities of the home. Astha had thought that Hemant would look after their children but Hemant considers this as 'a woman's work'. She expresses these feelings of alienation and grief through her poems. She wants to publish her poems but Hemant shows no interest in her plan.

Hemant is an agile businessman with foresight which has helped him establish a profitable business. Hemant behaves indifferently in his family which disappoints Astha. He considers that she is living an aimless life and has no destination to follow. When his business expands, Hemant goes frequently to foreign which makes Astha the virtual father as well as the mother of the children.

Astha knows that their relation has become very superficial, one that has lost genuineness because Hemant is too practical and devoid of any sympathy for her. She considers that marriage is not only a lifelong alliance but an institution that encompasses many other equations of life. All she wants is an understanding relationship with her husband. When Hemant discusses with her, he speaks very bitterly and invariably. His imperious virulent remarks cause disconnect so deep that she is thrown into an emotional swirl. All her aspirations are blurred. She is terribly alienated as her mother, in spite of all the members of her family around she struggles lonely with the agonies growing within her heart. Her personal conflict and emotional pain are unresolved matters that leave her appalled. An indifferent attitude of her husband and her inability to find a meaning in life are source of trouble to Astha. She wishes to maintain her own individuality than sacrificing and accommodative woman. She wants Hemant would have time to listen to her and validate what she feels. She realizes that one does not always need to have an answer for everything; just being each other and loving each other unconditionally can make a difference.

Astha's mother is living in an Ashram on the banks of the Ganga in Rishikesh. She mails her a small booklet along with a letter in which she advises her to hold firmly the life which seems to be slipping from her, she writes:

> Accept without condition if you want to live in piece.... In time of difficulty don't lose heart...accommodation and acceptance keep families together...create a home where you are. (83-84)

When she is lost and disillusioned, she looks for her mother's consoling words.

Astha finds it difficult to reconcile to the preaching of her mother. She hates Hemant's straightforward conduct with his parents. She suffers when her mother does not trust Hemant with her flat and possessions and when Hemant donates all her father's books to a library. She considers these acts as the conspiracy against her.

Living in a patriarchal tradition, Astha's mother considers that it is Hemant who can and must decide things and Astha is made to realize that the house belongs to Hemant. And she considers Astha incapable of handling certain issues. Astha thinks that she belongs to nowhere and has no place to call her own. Therefore, she faces always a question that 'then who am I?' She feels her situation is that of a useless person who can't change it. Other members in the family seek to realize that being a woman she has no natural claim in the property. She wants 'she had a house that was more clearly hers'. Even Hemant looked upon her mother's investments and other money matters after her father. Astha is subjugated in the patriarchal frame of the family for obvious reason except money and material things; he becomes possessive to other aspects of life. "The silent negation on Hemant's part made her stand up in self-defiance for she was not ready to submit to ignorance" (Singh, Alma 23).

To Astha life becomes chaotic and gloomy and therefore when she comes in contact with Aijaz Akhtar Khan, the founder of the Street Theater Group, she immediately develops a liking for him. Aijaz also admires Astha for her artistic talents. He is the teacher of history as well as a performer in theatre. He tries to remove the thoughts of homeliness and melancholy from the life of Astha and unfolds new world of love and assists her to develop into a woman of independence, confidence and enterprise. On the other hand, Hemant rarely took her talent seriously. Hemant never gives a patient ear to her thoughts and perception about life.

Aijaz's sudden death in a communal frenzy during Ramjanambhumi and Babri Masjid demolition disturb Astha and her intelligent views about Hindu Muslim co-existence. In spite of the gamut of frightening emotions, Astha continues working for and supporting the cause of the new society. Astha participates in rallies and is proud to be part of the Sampradayaka Mukti March. Hemant can't understand Astha's convictions and her slogging for the cause of the Munch. Though she crossed the threshold of neurosis, she realizes life is not all smooth sailing. If Aijaz comes into her life for a while, and is killed in a riot, she still dreams about love and sexual pleasure with him.

> That night as the pain receded and she fell asleep, she dreamt.... The person turned it was Aijaz with long silky hair, which brushed across her face.... Together, they walked in a room...slowly they fell on the bed, kissing all the while, when Aijaz, entwined around her. (*MW* 154-55)

To Sum Up

The male supremacy in the society intensifies the suppression of women as their relationship with their husbands reduces to be merely superficial and very little genuine. Astha considers her marital life emotionally unrealistic and unconvincing. She has been brought up in a conventional family set up. Marriage has been to her a shattered romantic dream. She dreams the dream of her marriage fulfilled in her unorthodox sexual way of life which is rather unconventional.

WORKS CITED

Judith, Stacy. *In the Name of the Family, Rethinking Family Values in the Postmodern Age*. Boston: Bacon Press, 1996.

Kapur, Manju. *A Married Woman,* New Delhi: India Ink, 2002.

Kumar, Ashok. Portrayal of New Woman: A Study of Manju Kapur's *A Married Woman, Indian Writing in English: Critical Ruminations,* Vol. II: Amar Nath Prasad and John Peter Joseph (eds.). New Delhi: Sarup and Sons, 2006.

Singh, Alka. A Tempting Trap: Manju Kapur's *A Married Woman, Contemporary Indian Writing in English: Critical Perceptions* NDR Chandra (ed.). New Delhi: Sarup and Sons, 2005.

Sinha, Shalini R. The Conflict between the Roots and Wings in Manju Kapur's *A Married Woman,* In *A Critical Perspectives, Indian Writing in English, Critical Rumination*, Vol. 1, Amar Nath Prasad and John Peter Joseph (eds.). New Delhi: Sarup and Sons, 2006.

11

Changing Image of Women in *Difficult Daughters*

Ashish Gupta

Manju Kapur is an Indian novelist born at Amritsar in 1948 graduated from the Miranda House, Delhi University and went on to take on M.A. at Dalhousie University Halifax Nova. She was a professor where she teaches English literature at Miranda House College, Delhi. She is presently living in Delhi. Her first novel *Difficult Daughters* won the 1999 Commonwealth Writers' Prize. Manju Kapur is well known for her sharp-eyed, catching her character portraits in tricky situations. When one reads her novel, a new significant meaning can be viewed of crisscross dogmas of cultural critical thinking. The life women lived and struggled under the oppressive mechanism of a closed society are reflected in her novels. Manju Kapur's novels present the changing image of women; moving away from traditional portrayals of enduring women, self-sacrificing women towards self-assured, assertive and ambitious women making society aware of their demands and in this way providing a medium of self-expression.

> One is not born but rather becomes a woman. No biological, psychological or economic fate determines the figure that the human female presents in society; it is civilization as a whole that produces this creature. (Beauvoir, Simon, 1949, *The Second Sex*)

The Indian woman is caught in flux of tradition and modernity saddled with burden of the past to cast off her aspirations. In the novels of Kapur, the women go through transitional phase where they become different from traditional women and want to tread new paths. The modern woman does not find any sense in such self-sacrifice and yearns for self-expression, individuality and self-identity. A woman is never regarded as a autonomous being since she has always been assigned a subordinate and a relative position.

Manju Kapur's novel *Difficult Daughters* (1999) focuses on sturdy self-assured women characters who raise anxiety and show courage and determination to apprehend their goals in life. This paper is an attempt to reveal profound insight of female's inner conflict and carve a way out of the dilemma in order to find an amicable solution. Women have been lagging behind in world literature for centuries. On the one hand, there are examples of Sita, Rani Laxmi Bai and others who have followed their own paths but on the other if one violates the traditional norms, one is subjected to bitter criticism by the society. Manju Kapur has realistically depicted the female consciousness in *Difficult Daughters* and tried to show the struggle a woman has to do in order to prove her identity in the male-dominated society. Virmati, the protagonist in *Difficult Daughters* struggles hard for her existential identity in adverse circumstances. The novelist has woven into text the story of three generations of the family in order to bring to fore the female exploitation not only by the male members but even by the female members.

Difficult Daughters is a novel set in pre-partition scenario of India. It is partially based on the life of Virmati. The story is woven with beautiful life-like characters. Novel is written across three generations. It's the story of 20th-century Punjabi family. The protagonist Virmati takes birth as a granddaughter here. The political and social issues are effectively woven in the story with the issues regarding women, education versus marriage. The novel opens with Ida, the daughter of Virmati who tries to find out the past of her mother which was always hidden from her. Ida comes to Amritsar to her relatives from where she is able to get all the past details. Virmati falls in love with her professor, who is already married and has two children. Even though he married Virmati and takes her to his home. Virmati's parents cut off all relation with her. Even at her new home, she obviously had bad term with professor's first wife. Soon she finds her way to get little freedom, by having further education with M.A. at Lahore. At the end of the novel, one can see India achieved freedom and even Virmati too was happy with professor at her home. She even had reconciliation with her family. Thus with the freedom struggle at the backdrop of the story, Virmati too had to fight for her study, her desire for marriage with her lover, and last she even felt the taste of wine of freedom, mentally, and socially.

Virmati finds herself in no position to reveal her love for professor to the family members who fix her marriage with an engineer: it seemed to Virmati that her family could talk of nothing else but her wedding. Every word they said had so little relation to her inner life that she felt fraudulent evening listening to them, "passively, immorally silent" (70). The woman has to undergo pain and torture in order to tackle the peculiar situation. But the norms of patriarchal social system do not allow her to expose her feelings of love in order to select a suitable man for her as her life partner. The old-fashioned mother Kasturi represents the generation that follows the fundamental dictum of society and is ready to sacrifice her daughter at the altar of marriage for good reputation and attach little importance to education of a girl:

> 'Please, I want to study...' Virmati faltered.
>
> 'But you have studied. What else is left?' 'In Lahore...I want to go to Lahore....'
>
> Kasturi could bear her daughter's foolishness no further. She grabbed her by the hair and banged her head against the wall.
>
> May be this will knock some sense into you! She cried. 'What crimes did I commit in my last life that I should be cursed with a daughter like you in this one?' (59)

This is how a woman stands against her daughter and forces her for marriage. "Remember you are going to be married next month, if I have to swallow poison to make you do it!" (60). Mother's only concern is her daughter's marriage. Virmati's firm determination for getting higher education becomes fruitful after she goes to drown herself in a bid of frustration and disillusionment. The family members realize the need of the hour and send her to Lahore in the company of her cousin Shakuntala who has been a source of inspiration for her by extending her a helping hand in critical moments of Virmati's life:

> You will find Viru that in Lahore people are not so narrow-minded. It is a pity the man was married, but you have done the right thing. Together we will face the family. After all I have experience in resisting pressures. Don't worry I am on your side. (115)

The family plays crucial role in many ways in the development or fall of a female. Virmati's family especially her mother behave rudely and confine her to a go down of the house like an animal in order to keep her away from the matrimonial ceremony of her sister's marriage. She is compelled to leave the house for the sake of her freedom and education in Lahore. Ida, Virmati's daughter represents modern woman that does not follow the traditional path blindly but chooses the rational approach to discover reality behind her mother's troublesome past. She is keen to visit the place where her mother 'was educated after so much trouble' in order to know the reality about her mother's past life:

> I want to see the place that had been the Mecca for all Punjabis. Lahore, where students gathered on the river, around the mausoleums, through the mall, in the gardens, the shopping areas, the eating places, the theatres. Where anybody with their brains went to study. To learn, to meet people, hear leaders, be in contact with social, political, fashionable trends. The centre of Punjab, its heart and soul, and how much else besides. (137)

Sense of emotional attachment to a man is a female's quality. Virmati's miserable plight is that she is in a fix to assess her real condition after being secretly married to Harish, the professor in Lahore.

The tremendous inner conflict in the novel is depicted in Virmati when she was at Lahore. She isolated herself from the place as some past memories with professor made her unable to move forward in life. She came at Lahore but professor chased her here also and again intimacy grew among them. Though she was getting the love but still she was confused with her own life. At Punjab Women's Student Conference, she was tapped in her own thought about her existence, and the importance she gave in her life. At this point she felt isolated by sitting there, and by listening to Mohini Datta's speech on how freedom was necessary for the human development of the human spirit, how war especially affected women, how progress was their object so that freedom could be enjoyed by all classes, etc. She wonders about herself, she quest inside her own mind,

> Am I free...I came here to be free, but I am not like these women. They are using their minds. Organizing, participating in conferences, politically active, while my time is spent being in love. Wasting it. Well, not wasting time, no, of course not, but then how come I never have a moment for anything else? (142)

Even after her marriage, the way she was treated at her husband's home make her feel insecure. She use to think over why can't she do all her husband's washing, cooking, clean his books, fill his pen with ink, all work which Ganga supposed to do. Even on the first day in her husband house she felt isolated which made her to give statement. "I should have never married you" (121).

The professor makes extramarital relationship with Virmati out of his deep love for her but the society in the form of wife, mother, and sister doesn't allow converting this relationship into marriage. And a girl has to undergo much humiliation and face difficulties due to patriarchal structure of society. Virmati realistically puts her real picture before her lover:

> I break my engagement because of you, blacken my family's name, am locked up inside my house, get sent to Lahore because no one knows what to do with me. Here I am in the position of being your secret wife, full of shame, wondering what people will say if they find out, not being able to live in peace, study in peace and why.... (149)

It is marriage which matters for a girl like Virmati who is not in a position to understand the real factor behind the excuse of delay in marriage ceremony. Indian social barriers and legal parameters don't permit a man to marry many times. After her involvement with Harish, Virmati realizes the fact that he wants to 'prolong the situation' of marriage. But soon after the marriage, the relationship appears as a mirage and starts underestimating herself. Virmati's marriage with a married professor was never acceptable and it was a great humiliating jolt for Lala Diwanchand's family. Followed by it there was her father's tragic death in a partition riot and due to the unbearable woe of son's sudden death, successive death occurs to Lala Diwanchand. Consequently, infuriated Kasturi totally shut down the doors for Virmati forever. All blood relations from her parental home at Lepel Griffin Road seems cold and barren to Virmati. She realizes that all ties between herself and her family are broken. The relations were strained and broken to the extent that she was not even invited for her brother's marriage, though even most remote relatives were invited. Thus, she fails to create a space for herself for which she had been striving all along. Kapur aims at projecting through her protagonist that when an Indian young girl marries according to her own choice. It spoils her prospects in both the worlds. So there was also the partition line drawn by Virmati between her and family and same partition caused by her in the integrated family of the professor.

Through the story Kapur criticizes the mentality of society. Society accepts man's guilt and also forgives him but that not happen about woman. Manju Kapur wants to tell how Virmati and Ida become difficult daughters without any mistake of their parents. Gopal and Virmati both fall in love but the punishment bears on Virmati. They focus on characters, aptness of title, tradition and transformation as well as study a novel in feminist approach. This book is excellent for the scholars and students for their study. The writer has done the study of novel *Difficult Daughters* in different angels. The focus of the book is mainly on the life of Virmati and her relationship with father, mother, sister as well as her own daughter. She is a second wife and her agonies are realistically presented in this novel.

Due to the uneven illness and incessant pregnancy of her mother, as an elder daughter in the family, much of the domestic responsibility has been shouldered by Virmati in her family. But while playing the role of a second mother to her ten siblings, frequently there were nerves of youth phase like grievances, irritations and strong reactions reflected by Virmati to her mother. These familial responsibilities in her tender teenage youth appear and confront to Viru as impediments and predicaments in her craving for higher education. She has been depicted as a teenage young girl of modern generation with tremendous academic pursuit. That is why for Kasturi her daughter appears as an enigmatic type of personality. There was a kind of eruption like a volcano in the mind of young Viru, who was always fidgeting to achieve something noble which will illuminate her life and cherish a dream of education. Kasturi always wondered as to why was her daughter so restless all the time? But due to the generation gap she could not pierce in-depth in the inner mind of her daughter. Thus, Viru appears as an emerging teenage youth, who does not want to be a 'rubber doll' or 'puppet' for others to move as they wished. On an occasion Kasturi realizes her teenaged daughter, awakening in her responsibilities of life. As she says: "At your age I was already expecting you, not fighting with my mother" (19). So this statement indicates the problem of generation gap, which arises between mother and young daughter. It symbolizes as one of the conflicting aspects in the social life.

This book is an aroma of female struggle in modern India. The writer shows that how Virmati wanted to lead life on her own accord. Virmati being a simple girl emancipate herself and fight for her goal for her education and love. The writer has given the minute details about her suffering while leading a life. This book shows that while leading life how female characters of this novel become difficult daughters for their parents. The article concludes on the point that Virmati becomes really a difficult daughter for her parents and her daughter Ida also become the same to her parents. Virmati is a model and representative of new woman. Virmati who is portrayed with great sympathy and warmth to cloud our colonial consciousness. Virmati's fight is against the rules made for women by male. Her suffering relates to the vital issues of modern women and their emancipation. She is caught between family duty and love for education as well as for her illegitimate love with married man. She accepts her suffering with great fortitude and fight for education and economic independence gives her new thinking power.

In her protagonist, Kapur has dexterously mingled the complex and convoluted emotions of guilt and cravings, drive and regression, clarity, and confusion. Obviously, it reflects the predominant characteristics of modern Indian young generation woman. With the strong aspirations and determinations, in mind, the protagonist, Virmati was craving to move forward by keeping the pace with modern world by overcoming traditional orthodox ideas on the right track of education as her sole destination. The novel has been written against the backdrop of the Indian freedom movement, the partition of India and the Second World War between Allied and Axis forces. Manju Kapur focuses our attention to the fact of fast changing scenario from the view point of women when they can participate even in the freedom struggle and the activities like education for the sake of their better future.

To conclude, Manju Kapur has vividly presented the life of women struggling against the patriarchal system of society in order to claim her right place. The novel is rather a story of a woman's continuous struggle for her existential identity against the perception of domesticity. The novel is the miserable tale of a woman torn between her family responsibility, the passion for education and her illicit love. The novel touches myriad issues like revolt against deep-rooted family tradition, the search for self-hood women's rights, marriage, gender discrimination, and battle for independence at both fronts personal and national. The novel depicts the triumph of the women's spirit, her longing to beat the odds, to conquer weaknesses and to move forward. Manju Kapur's novel *Difficult Daughters* thus present the changing image of women; moving away from traditional portrayals of enduring women, self-sacrificing women towards self-assured. assertive and ambitious women making society aware of their demands and in this way providing a medium of self-expression.

WORK CITED

Kapur, Manju. *Difficult Daughters*. New Delhi: Penguin Books India (P) Ltd., 1999.

All subsequent references in parentheses are from this edition of the novel.

12

Marriage as Taboo: A Study on Jai Nimbkar's *Temporary Answer*

R. Soundararajan

From the past to the present, the existence of woman has always been regarded as being subordinate to man. Of course, now, the structures of the society and the ways of women's subordination have changed due to the different political and the social ideologies. Now there is an awareness of our society that this marginalization of women, besides being a great discrimination, cuts at the every roots of democratic life itself. So, the protest of women against this inequality has resulted in the formation of various women's liberation movements and now there is also a well-articulated 'dogma' for this liberation which takes the name of 'feminism'. In fact, this concept has come into existence as a result of the realization, by women themselves, about their power and status and it has made the society to revise the norms which, so far, have considered women as only the 'second sex'.

Indian English writers have begun to articulate women's aspirations for equality as well as respect in the society. Especially, post-colonial Indian women novelists have achieved greater success than man, by bringing a greater emphasis to this problem of women's emancipation by their imaginative recreation of it in their fiction which has now obviously seen.

Women novelists like Kamala Das, Anita Dasai, Shashi Deshpande, Jai Nimbkar, Kamala Markandaya, Githa Hariharan, Nayantara Sahgal, Bharati Mukherjee, Shobhaa De, Arundhati

Roy, Anita Manjoshi, Rama Mehta, etc. have portrayed their women characters with courage to fight for their emancipation and empowerment. Almost every writer has accepted the feminist theory against the oppression of women and have used it as a given and as a reference point in their application to literature. Without any shilly-shallying, readers can say that Indian English feminist writers have created a new breadth to Indian English fiction. They have made a new path to reconstruct the 'new woman', who is liberated, intelligent and strong enough to perform all that men can do.

Among them, Jai Nimbkar is a prominent feminist writer, who through her three novels has tried to depict almost every aspect of the social problem. By her novels—*Temporary Answers* (1947), *A Joint Venture* (1988), and *Come Rain* (1993), she has thrived on portraying her unfathomable social concern over the gender-bias shown by the patriarchy. Her women protagonists are victims of patriarchy but they are intelligent enough to analyze their problems critically and brave enough to fight against all evils, asserting their individuality and identity, without, however, denying the other identity of man. Marriage, they decide at last, is merely a temporary answer for their loneliness, if there is no love among the two partners. Woman is a person and, as a woman, she always needs a man as her companion for life but, as a person, she deserves her freedom and individuality.

Marriage is a consensual and contractual relationship recognized by law. As Indian traditional cultural ideology concerned, marriage is a sacred union between the male and the female, which unites them spiritually as well as emotionally. The Hindus have idealized marriage in a big way. In the patriarchal society of Vedic Hindus, marriage was considered as a sacramental union, and this continued to be so during the entire period. In the *Shastric Hindu Law* (Diwan, 72), marriage has been regarded as one of the essential *sanakaras* (sacrament for every Hindu). For a Hindu, marriage is essential, not only for begetting a son in order to discharge his debt to the ancestors, but also for performance of other religious and spiritual duties. The sacramental aspect of marriage under Hindu law has three characteristics: (1) That it is a sacrament union, which means that marriage is not to gratify one's physical needs; but is primarily meant for the performance of religious and spiritual duties; (2) a sacramental union implies that a marriage once entered cannot be dissolved on any ground whatsoever; and (3) a sacramental union also means that it is a union of soul, body, and mind. It is a union not only for this life, but for all lives to come. The union is not only for this world, but also for other worlds. The institution of marriage is considered sacred even by those who view it as a civil contract.

But in the modern era there is a tremendous social and cultural pressure to marry. It is of paramount importance to discuss the relationship between marriage and mental illness in Indian scenario as marriage is perceived to be a panacea to mental illness by many. Biological dichotomization is there in all forms of life and it is a natural law for male and female elements to unite for the propagation of life. In lower forms of life, this union is temporary and casual. But as the human beings belong to higher organism, so they follow certain rules and regulations which become social traditions and norms. This includes woman as the weaker sex and man as the stronger sex. Hence, the concept of marriage under the modern perception especially in the Indian context is full of absurdity.

The prescription of marriage is more stringent for women. Women must get married. "*Doosre ki amanat hai*" (She is another person's property). "*Jawan ladki ghar nahin baitha sakte hain*" (cannot keep a young unmarried girl at home). After marriage, her husband's home is her home. She should visit her natal home only as a guest, she should never return to her parents' home. Parents cough out their life savings too/take loans/dispose of their property and arrange for substantial dowry to marry their daughters. In India, marriage and family dominate the life of women. The primary duty of a woman is to be subservient/loyal to the husband/his relatives and her children. After marriage, husband and relatives control all outside relationships.

Jai Nimbkar as one among the eminent feminist writers delineates feminism in all her three novels. In these she has portrayed woman in her quest for identity, who struggles with all the hurdles and the rigidity of the social system. To show this quest the author very meticulously deals with the theme of marriage in the Indian context. Dr. J.M. Waghmare says,

> Jai Nimbkar's fiction is characterized by feminism, no doubt. But the world of her female characters ultimately ends not with a bang, but a whimper. The cultural condition of Indian women is, by and large, responsible for this pathetic situation. (17)

Thus, the protagonists aspire to get something unique from their life, and their desire ultimately succeeds for them to realize their identity fully. Nimbkar's female characters approach as integrated individuals who very well synthesize both personal and social lives in a harmonious way. She successfully depicts the oppressed and suppressed condition of the women in the so-called underdog society. She reinforces the female dilemma in the discourse to get equal opportunities. Indian women always try to realize their identity within the confines of the socio-cultural milieu.

In her novels, Jai Nimbkar depicts traditions and customs of Indian marriage system which often become weapons to attack women's liberation itself. So marriage often stands for the subversion and social obliteration of women. The author here also highlights the question of widow remarriage, which creates an ambivalent attitude in the protagonist Vineeta in *Temporary Answers*. She feels that by marrying again her female identity may be in a stake. Jyoti, in *A Joint Venture*, is a married woman, who is denied her identity by her husband, in the beginning, but later realizes her identity. For thirty long years, she worked as a sleeping partner in her husband's seed business which he managed by himself and in the game she never had any chance to enjoy the natural pleasure of even motherhood. Her children got themselves far from parents, as her husband was a dominating person who never cared for her feelings or decisions and now she is alone. So marriage now seems to be a frustrating venture for her. But at last she returns to her husband to support him in his bad conditions. The Indian woman is long suffering but she can never tolerate to her husband's lack of respect. So this saga of a 'marriage' is very carefully crafted by Mrs. Nimbkar who, in fact, uses different words for marriage such as 'temporary answer', 'joint venture', 'tricky game', and 'weapon against women's liberation', etc. Anyway, the author is not directly against the system of marriage but she wants to depict that there should be love and mutual respect in between the couple, and then only it will fulfill all meanings of marriage.

Jai Nimbkar sketches her female protagonists in such a way that they never spoil the bliss of their marital status. But always these new women get their middle way out to solve their problems intelligently. They are neither meek nor weak, nor do they compromise and succumb to the male patriarchy. Nimbkar is a very conscious writer that she never allows her female characters to cross the boundaries socially of the plutonic relationship. Vineeta, Jyoti, and Ann are the three central female protagonists of her three different novels. They face all hurdles of their life very boldly and very intelligently and achieve their aim to get their identity. They are able to control their emotions and set up a smooth pleasurable life before any damage is done to their harmonious lives. Moreover, these women do not want to harm other's freedom or identity in their journey to get their own. No doubt, they are strong and determined but they achieve their will after a conscious analysis of each and every aspect of life. They think in all directions, into the past, onto the present and into the future as well.

In the beginning of the novel, *Temporary Answers,* the protagonist Vineeta cannot avoid the socio-cultural milieu but faces bravely her misfortune of a sudden and early widowhood. Vineeta's keen observation of married relations makes her to wake up, to be emotionally independent. She feels marriage and love are all only temporary answers to avoid her loneliness, unless and until there is equality and respect between the couple.

Dr. A.P. Dani, in his article "Jai Nimbkar's Temporary Answers: A Unified World of Transience", writes,

> Vineeta undergoes vicissitudes of relationships in her personal, domestic and professional life to realize that love and marriage, unless based on equality, freedom, trust and self-respect, will continue to be temporary answer to her problems and frustrations. (3)

As a typical Indian culture-based Vineeta who has possessed education on medicine, without any expectations agrees the marriage proposal when Nagendra has proposed to her. He too has all that an ordinary Indian girl would wish for in a husband. But only in later stage that reality bit into her and made her realize in what purpose he really wants to marry her. It is his sense of ownership that has come into play. He would be proud to possess a doctor as wife and to display her as a showpiece to his numerous friends.

> He would have thought it a matter of prestige if his wife was a practicing doctor. He told me he was attracted to me because I was different from the other girls he knew, because had a sense of direction. (22)

Vineeta was so happy in her early days of marriage. Nagendra fulfilled her every want and wish: he talked to her pleasantly and made much of her. They enjoyed each other's company fully at home. Vineeta was so swamped with the marriage that she readily tried to learn to fit into the scheme that her husband had for her. "Nagendra had his group and the same faces turned up everywhere. I tried to feel part of them but couldn't. Learn to be like them outwardly.... But I rebel against it all" (23). So, together with acquiescence and consonance, the act of insurrection also began to draw within her soul. She thought she gave herself in completely to Nagendra but she didn't get much of him in return. Of course, Nagendra sensed her state of rebellion but did not decide to fight it out as he was not a violent man by nature. He merely ignored her.

> So we had bitter fights. Or no, that's not an accurate description. It was I who fought, I who hurled accusations at him. He was comparatively calm because he was not really involved in the issue I fought over.... I was not a very important part of his life. (92)

On one Sunday, a holiday which Vineeta would like to spend with her husband, her husband insisted her to attend his friend's marriage party. Instead of going along with her husband, she would be completely bold in the company of Nagendra's male friends. Anyway, without giving any consideration for Vineeta's wish Nagendra decided to go alone to the party and spend almost his whole day with his male friends. Besides, after the party he went on to visit his aged parents at their home. Vineeta who wanted to spend at least some part of the holiday with Nagendra thought that he could have visited his parents on another evening. She was offended by the behaviour of Nagendra.

> I cried because it was impossible for me to reach him. I considered committing suicide. I took a lot of pleasure in imagining his shocked disbelieve when be came home and saw me dead. (94)

Nagendra returned late at night, made love to her as usual and went to sleep as if there was nothing the matter. "The next morning he did not even refer to the incident the last word bad been said about it, as far as he was concerned. He was cheerful and affectionate and I could only feel bruised and beaten" (94). Then all of it, at once came to an end. A sudden heart attack of Nagendra put an end to her married life. There was no immediate cause for the sudden heart attack as otherwise his health was excellent and as he was careful to maintain it with rest and exercise. Characteristically, Vineeta took upon herself the blame for the sudden turn of events. She now thought that perhaps he was trying to change over to a new way of life with his marriage and that it was her fault that she was unable to understand it and to cooperate with him.

The novel opens with her widowhood, showing the emptiness in the heroine's life after the sudden death of her husband. It is because in India the socio-cultural conditions make the widow an outcast. Society looks down upon a widow. She refuses her mother to attend her cousin's thread ceremony. She says: "I just don't feel like facing all relatives.... I did not say there was anything wrong with them. I just don't enjoy the idea of meeting all of them at once, that's all" (9). This made her to become so negative and diffident in herself so that she does not even take up practice as a doctor. The culture which has ingrained in her soul was pushing her back from moving or even thinking to move forward.

Vineeta who is a luckless disconcerted petrified but assertive and courageous woman returns to her parents in Poona and starts later her career as a pediatrician. She faces intricacies of relationships in her personal, professional and domestic life. In order to find peace with herself and occupation, and purpose of life, she accepts voluntary work of social welfare. But as a widow trying to encounter and reconcile with her misfortune, she is unable to choose for her life partner again between Vilas, as old-time friend of hers and fellow doctor, and Abhijit, a college professor and playwright. She has rejected the proposal of marrying Vilas who loves her; she cannot requite his love. Her sister Madhuri, a flippant flirt, succeeds curiously in winning over Vila's hand in marriage and warns her that now Vineeta has no claim on Vilas because it was lost when she refused to marry him and that she has no right to come between them and try to break up their marriage.

Vineeta loves Abhijit and confides in him all her problems and frustrations but does not experience the reciprocity from him for which she has been waiting patiently. She wants an equal relationship with him. Her acceptance of marriage is conditional. She holds, "we must stand alone, complete in ourselves before we could meet in marriage. I could not remain lame, crippled only half a person and expect him always lend me support, the illusion of wholeness" (173). She wants Abhijit "to give her a real chance to deal with her problems in her own way and trust her capacity to do so" (175) rather than to adopt a patronizing and condescending attitude of protectiveness to her from death and disintegration. In fact, she has rejected Vilas because she believes that "he would be the sort of husband who would treat a wife like a fragile thing which requires protection, smother her with good things in life and be genuinely baffled is she rebelled against playing the role of a household pet" (151). She is infatuated with Abhijit and asks for his help. He intends to help her by loving her. He discloses to her, "You know I love you, don't you?" (178). Vineeta considers this as "only a *temporary answer*". Abhijit rejoins, "That's all we have, *temporary answers*. What more can you ask for?" Vineeta is satisfied for the time being with this 'temporary answer'. Her mother who is a nagging and domineering woman in the family advises her to get married to Professor Abhijit Gokhale. Vineeta argues that she does not want "to rush into marriage" and find out that "her husband is a man she cannot respect or love" (179). Her mother asserts, "...marriage has its faults, but a woman can't live her life alone. She needs the protection of a man, the security that only marriage can offer her and warns her that she would find some day that her mother was right" (182). Her mother has an incise perception of her daughter's character. She asserts, "The trouble with you, Vineeta, is that you expect too much of yourself. That's because you think too much of yourself. You were always like this" (182). But what Vineeta aspires for, is the prevalence of her lost control over herself and thus the control of the world. That is perhaps the explanation why "she had never been able to say it easily" that she loved Abhijit. She tells him that she did not like to use the word love until she was sure both of them meant the same thing by it. She would like to attain maturity, peace, marked individuality and legitimate self-respect before she wants to get married to Abhijit.

To conclude, Vineetha feels that her love for Abhijit is only an extension of her self-love, and expression of her anxiety about herself. She realizes that love which is supposed to have sensitized her to Abhijit, whom she loves, has actually sensitized her to herself. This self-love prevents her from judging the situation objectively, steadily and as a whole. Her indecision, irresoluteness and puerile peevishness stem from this self-pity and self-love. Even her work for social service has not been with unmixed identification and dedication. It fulfills the mutual need. She believes, "we lived in different worlds and they belonged very much to their world and I to mine. There was no overlapping. But I fulfilled a need in their lives and they in mine. Wasn't that enough?" (185). So, Vineeta now tells Abhijit to treat her no more as a child and leave her to fight her battles Abhijit. "I said, 'Abhijit, do you understand? You must go away. You must let me handle with my problems in my own way. You must trust me'". Abhijit fully understand love the meaning of her words that both of them should now travel separately on a journey together their independent strength, for some time, so that finally they could be united as fully realized person into the unity of love.

WORKS CITED

Borate, T.S. 1995. "Jai Nimbkar's A Joint Venture: A Study in Feminine-Feminist-Female Consciousness", *Indian Women Novelists*, R.K. Dhawan, Prestige Books, New Delhi, Set III, Vol. 4: 84.

Diwan P. *Modern Hindu Law.* Allahabad: Allahabad Law Agency, 2008.

Nimbkar, Jai. *Temporary Answers.* New Delhi: Disha Books, 1947.

Pawar, M.S. *New Women Novelists with New Horizon.* Jaipur: Shruti Publication, 2011.

Vyas, A. Manish. *Ideological Conflict and Assertion in Jai Nimbkar's Come Rain Contemporary Indian Writers.* Ed. S.M. Ali. Jaipur: Mark Publisher, 2004.

Waghmare, J.M. "Foreward", R.S. Ratnam (ed.), *Critical Essays on Indian Women Writing in English.* New Delhi: Harman Publishing House, 1999.

13

Sexual Violence in the Spiritual Sanctuary: A Study of Anuradha Roy's *Sleeping on Jupiter*

N. Velmani

If women are to discover and express who they are, they must begin with their sexuality and obviously it begins with their bodies. Female body becomes the site of forced colonization which the male master not only uses but also their target of assault and abuses. Luce Irigaray rightly claims that "It is important for us to guard and keep our own bodies and at the same time make them emerge from the silence and subjugation" (421).

Women writers of today have moved away from traditional portrayal of women as enduring, self-sacrificing women, the characterization of gender inequalities, extra-marital relationship, rather, their novels discuss burning issues of contemporary reality, the cultural change, cyber culture due to the onset of globalization. A number of diasporic writers—postcolonial migrant writers of the first generation and second generation to the present young writers of the millennium—Jhumpa Lahiri, Kiran Desai, Tulsi Badrinath, Padma Viswananthan, Suma Chitnis, Aruna Chakravarti, Shilpa Agarwal, Veena Das, Malavika Karlekar, Kum Kum Sanjari, Anuradha Roy, Dina Mehta, Kalpana Swaminathan—work on the reality of women's issues and the contemporary aspects of Indian society not bothering only with patriarchy and gender biases. The recent film *India's Daughter* propagandas the hot news of the media the gruesome incident of a medical student gang raped.

Woman is doubly colonized both by Nature and man. The basic question asked by Draupadi in *The Mahabharata,* 'is woman a being or a thing?' still remains unanswered. Women's bodies are objectified by various means for male consumption and sexual declaration. Marriage becomes almost an institution enslaving women to a lifetime of male domination: "Marriages never end, they cannot—they are a state of being" (*That Long Silence* 127).

There's been a recent stormy call to action against sexual assault in India as rape cases have begun to make international headlines rather than being accepted as part of everyday female experience in the country. On the wake of this perpetration of violence against women and children, Roy's book *Sleeping on Jupiter* is timely released with extremely brave perspective. Roy in her "Acknowledgements" expresses,

> There are countless horrific cases of child abuse and sexual violence in India. I have drawn on the legal and investigative history of many such incidents...violence, being the LSD of our times, human interest stories on the subject play out one evening high-pitched news capsules in television every day. (II)

Anuradha Roy takes such a newspaper headline and turns it into the theatrical performance. *Sleeping on Jupiter* is a courage book dealing with a timely subject—violence against women within the most unexpected walls. The intriguing title comes from the protagonist's quest, their sense of being trapped in their lives and looking for alternative universe. "One, a temple guide, finds himself at such a crossroads that he yearns for the solitude of a totally different world. For him this becomes a longing to sleep on Jupiter under its 16 moons" (26).

There is a tapestry of lost innocence, displacement, rejection and pain in Roy's latest novel *Sleeping on Jupiter.* Her first book *The Folded Earth* was set around plateaus and rivers, the second novel *Atlas of Impossible Longing* was set in the hills, the third novel *Sleeping on Jupiter* is set by the sea Jarmuli, a made-up fictional place, convincing complex location for the novel. Originally, the book started as a long short story. She then started following incidental characters, particularly a girl on a beach and an elderly tea-seller.

> Unpeeling the layers of their stories led me to unexpected directions. The narrative lends itself to jagged edges, spliced narrative and areas of mystery, so I structured it in a radically different way from my two earlier books. (45)

The story occurs across a prologue-like chapter documenting a violent past and then a chapter each across the 18 days, the various protagonists spend by the sea, unravelling their present. The scenes are so vivid, the first murder, the loss-of-innocence, the sea temple visit, the violence pin-pointing a real event and Nomi, the girl who is made a refugee to be an Everywoman horribly affected from wars and violence.

Nomita Frederikson from Oslo is travelling to Jarmuli to make a documentary on the temple town. But she has an unspoken reason for her journey. Vidya, Latika, and Gowri, senior citizens and close friends are travelling to Jarmuli in the same A2 compartment. They are concerned about the solitary young girl when she is attacked as she gets off the train. They can do nothing and watch from inside. The train leaves but they don't pull the chain. They are destined to 'meet' later, by the sea are Badal Raghu and Johnny Tepo, trapped in a life not of their choice.

The context of the novel takes place over five days in the coastal temple town of Jarmuli in contemporary India. The town is populated ostensibly by priests and pilgrims and it is popularly known as a spiritual sanctuary, evil, and brutality appear to trump goodness and innocence at every turn. Roy interweaves gracefully a lot of characters—a young woman, all braided hair, tattoos and piercings; Nomita Frederiksen, a refugee from her adoptive Norway; Badal, the temple guide; a trio of elderly Calcutta ladies holidaying together, Vidya, Latika, Gowri; Suraj, her photographer accompanying her on the filming assignment to Jarmuli; Johnny Tepo, the chaiwala on the beach.

Nomi's pilgrimage and her travel to Jarmuli to pay homage to the famous temple is an attempt to confront the traumas of her past; Nomi is both Indian and non-Indian, having come from Norway: "The sun was like a moon in this country and in its light I felt as if I was looking at everything through a pearl" (11). She is transported with other orphaned refugee girls to the internationally celebrated coastal Jarmuli to seek the spiritual home and protection of Guruji "Who could see into me through my tunic and my skin and bones, right inside" (57). As the train continues on its way, her fate unknown to her motherly travelling companions "their holiday spirits snuffed out by the absence of a girl they knew not at all" (62)—until they encounter her a few days later in Jarmuli.

She disembarked at a station en route, to buy some bread and tea from a stand on the platform but within minutes, the three old women see the girl running for her life after being aggressively accosted by two men. The story is told in flashback how six years of her childhood were spent living in an ashram, a spiritual sanctuary populated by pilgrims and their protocols, the tourists and their guides, priests, and sadhus headed by a godman. When the guru was publically lauded all over the world, when the outside world wasn't watching, he inflicted emotional, physical, and sexual abuse on Nomi and other children in his care.

Anuradha Roy juxtaposes the sexual violence with the physical violence. A 7-year-old-child witnesses the murder of her father by axe-wielding masked men who have invaded their home. The smell of a ripe grape fruit fresh from their garden is contrasted with the sight of the whitewashed wall inside their hut 'streamed red' with the father's blood and the echoes of his haunting screams as he is beaten by the miscreant and then butchered like the pigs slaughtered for their meat. The horror and barbarity of Nomi's physical violence inhumanly echoes the palpable helpless anguish of three women physically separated by the window. The novelist focuses on the sexual violence juxtaposed with carving of the temple evoking carnal desires. The town's temple depicts the carvings of lovers coupled in a variety of embraces inciting sexual pleasure. The guide explains to the tourists: "Nothing wrong. Please understand. In ancient India no barrier between life and love. Erotic is creation itself, so it is celebrated in our temples" (103).

Sleeping on Jupiter revolves around the ethic and aesthetic instinct of lost and found concept—something oddly pleasing and anxiety—inducing that marks midnight thriller watching on television. In her list of acknowledgements, Roy weaves a common thread from the *Ramayana* and the *Mahabharata* and Jibanananda Das's poem *Bonolata Sen* and binds these texts with her novel. Das's famous poem is about a lover's search for the lost Bonolata Sen. Rama loses his wife to find her later; in the *Mahabharata*, the Pandavas lose their kingdom, property and wife and the Kauravas lose their lives. That is why Anuradha Roy places her novel by the sea, that ultimate metaphor for lost and found. Nomi feels,

> It's the sea. The sound of it. It brought back so many old things I had forgotten.... At every sea, she would sit down like this and wait for it to tell her something, she didn't know what, but she'd know it when it came. (87)

Roy scatters 'losses' throughout the novel—The novel begins with the death of Nomi's biological family, her mother, her brother, her childhood companion Piku and even her childhood. When Nomi arrives in India from Norway, to collect what has been lost, she gets lost herself. Suraj, the photographer who accompanies her on this filming assignment to Jarmuli, has lost his wife to his best friend; Badal, the guide, loses his scooter, a lover and almost his sanity; Tepo, the chaiwala on the beach, has lost his life as Jugnuin the ashram; of the three elderly women, one lost her husband to a secretary, another a Konkani lover and the third, a victim of dementia, her memory. The young Nomi says about her move from Jarmuli to Norway: "I was a parcel being sent from one country to another" (112).

In the modern feminist writing, a woman's body has acquired in-depth socio-cultural significations. It attempts to inscribe the internal or psychic engravings upon a woman's body which is the ultimate site of self-realization and true liberation. According to Judith Butler, the modern feminist, gender, sex, and gender identities are culturally constructed whereas sexuality along with sex is equally performative in nature. In her book *Bodies That Matter*, she writes "For surely body live and die; eat and sleep; feel pain and pleasure, endure illness and violence, and these 'facts'...cannot be dismissed as mere construction" (11).

The patriarchal perception of women as mute sex objects and mere bodies for sexual gratification is exposed through the novel. In spite of women's education and the career-oriented lifestyle of the current generation; woman has been commercialized as an amorous commodity and a prey to appease man's voluptuous desires. The novel successfully traces the grotesqueness and grossness.

Indian English fiction especially by feminist writers, gains significance in the sense that they outrageously question the commoditization of women as mere 'bodies'. They protest against the projection of women as mute sex objects that demean their dignity as human beings. Since the concept of sexuality has been essentially a male paradigm, the hegemonic value system expects women community to assimilate the indignity and feign silence and secrecy in controversial episodes like rape and sexual abuses.

WORKS CITED

Butler, Judith. *Bodies That Matter.* New York: Routledge, 1993.

Roy, Anuradha. *Sleeping on Jupiter.* New Delhi: OUP, 2015.

Sinha, Sunita (ed.). *Modern Literary Theory: New Perspectives.* New Delhi: Atlantic Publishers (P) Ltd., 2012.

Rivkin, Julie and Michael Ryan (ed.). *Literary Theory: An Anthology.* Malden: Blackwell Publishing, 2004.

www.thehindu.com/books/literary review Suniitha Balakrishnan.

14

Marginalization in the Select Novels of Meena Alexander

C. Shanmuga Priya

Indian Writing in English has always explored human values and their relevance in moments of crisis throughout the ages. From its very beginning, it has been focusing on social issues with Mulk Raj Anand being the pioneer of Indian Revolutionary novels in English. Treading in his path, the contemporary Indian writers in English especially women writers have focused on the theme of marginalization to the core. Many women who have moved to the West from India either as professional or as accompanying spouses have contributed substantially to expatriate literature in English. Their works describe colonial and postcolonial experiences from the angle of feminine sensibility of multiple marginalization with patriarchal constraints and as strangers in an alien Western society (Anita Singh 2009). One among them who is at her best is Meena Alexander, one of the recent South Asian American immigrant writers who depicts the social reality of conflict between the powerful and the powerless, and treats the downtrodden humanistically. Having faced lots and lots of mishappening in her childhood, she has dwelt upon the theme of marginalization in her novels in a very realistic manner. Hence, she has been hailed as "a poet and one of the finest thinkers of Asian American Aesthetic" (Dhawan and Neerja Chand 2001).

The theme of marginalization can be dealt with, under three levels, namely individual, communal and global levels. One could find traces of all these three levels of treatment of marginalization in the novels of Meena Alexander. Marginalization at the individual level ends up in an individual's exclusion especially women from participation in family and society. Communal marginalization includes a group or a community being deprived of any opportunity and suppressed with iron hand degrading their social stature. Global marginalization comprises the seclusion of a community as immigrants in the other world, feeling a sort of loneliness or incompatibility in the face of an alien land.

Meena Alexander began her literary career writing poetry, fiction, memoirs, and literary criticism. Irrespective of the genre, the anguish of people in different parts of the world has been articulated by her in a contemporary idiom. She obtained her doctorate in 1973 from the University of Khartoum (Alam 2006). She is known as a great poet basically with "the feminization of poetic discourse through thematic emphasis, choice of image and symbol, women person as and a significant use of "birthing metaphors" thronging her poetic writings (Jain et al., 2001). Though Meena has entered late to fiction after some years of writing poetry, she feels a great sense of energy and excitement from her fiction writing (Perry, 1995).

Meena Alexander's novels, *Nampally Road, Manhattan Music* and *Fault Lines—A Memoir* deal with the theme of marginalization at their best. Individual marginalization in all the three novels underlines the loneliness of the individual characters especially the protagonists of the novels. In her first novel, *Nampally Road,* Meena highlights how Mira the protagonist, is torn between her love for Ramu and her societal consciousness. Mira likes his protest against the political oppression but she feels herself being isolated and avoided by Ramu despite her love and support for him. Being a lecturer in English in Sona Nivas College, Hyderabad, she struggles to reconcile her two worlds—the world of her teaching of Tintern Abbey which has nothing to do with the pain and end up in the violence of modern India only to conclude that Wordsworth will really have to wait (Desiraju 1992). To her, poetry writing "seem the mere fruits of bourgeois privacy and the world of political activism" (Sanga 2003). She finds solace in her physical relationship with Ramu, though it does not end up in wedlock. When Ramu leaves Rameeza Be the rape-victim with Mira and disappears, she seems to accept reality with resignation. Laura Ribaldo, the immediate neighbor of Mira suffers in the hands of her drunkard husband Henry through his beatings. The physician, Pithulbai's daughter Maitreyi works as a menial servant sweeping the floors of the police station or to earn a living by selling snake poison as her father was compelled to sell her dowry to the Nizam for a handful of turmeric. *Manhattan Music* has its protagonist, Sandhya Rosenblum, a black woman married to a white man feeling marginalized as wife and as daughter-in-law sensing incompleteness of her marriage with Stephen in America. Muriel, the mother-in-law of Sandhya seems to agonize her telling her that she has to cope with Manhattan and with her American husband. Sandhya is often haunted by the memories of her former husband, Gautam and Delhi. She is often reminded of her mother Sarah's intervention in selecting the groom for her, careless of Sandhya's desire due to which Sandhya has hurt her forehead hitting it against the bathroom window asking, "why not kill me, if you want to dictate my life?" (*Manhattan Music* 26). Her friend, Smita has been burnt dreadfully in her newly married home by being harassed by her husband Rahul and her in-laws to get dowry. Rahul remarries after Smita's death. While Stephen's friend Draupati and his cousin Zeinab have been jilted by Rashid, an Egyptian, Sandhya shares her bed with him but to face the same predicament of those two women. She goes to the extent of hanging herself but rescued by Draupadi, who abhorts the child she begets from Rinaldo who denies to accommodate them. *Fault Lines—A Memoir,* the autobiography of Meena Alexander throws light on the author's childhood incidents of marginalization in Khartoum, Sudan, and Kerala. She captures the true picture of how girls were devoid of mirrors in schools to prevent 'the sin of vanity'. They would go snooping around for pools of water to find their faces. She could remember how girls were not allowed to go to get their higher education or to choose the life partner. Married women should have their heads covered with Katau sari before their in-laws. Meena had never been allowed to play with a woodcutter's child or a milkman's child.

Meena Alexander has amazingly brought in communal marginalization in all the three novels. *Nampally Road* revolves around many women characters who try to emerge with confidence in spite of the atrocities piled upon them. It totally represents the post-independent India and reflects the social conditions in Hyderabad when Emergency was declared by the then Prime Minister Mrs. Indira Gandhi in 1975. The gang-rape of a poor Muslim lady, Rameeza Be who comes with her husband to watch the movie *Isak Katha* shows the political brutality against the helpless woman. Her husband, Mohammad is beaten to death and thrown into the well by the drunken police. They drag the destitute woman to the Gowliguda police station where she is gang-raped by them. They shut her in a mud cell full of flies and mosquitoes. Her face is covered with blood stains and her whole body with bruises. This leads to communal riots and the people set ablaze the police station. Though the miscreants are jailed, violence is triggered outside and there is protest everywhere against the tyranny of police. The 'Ever-ready men', the henchmen of Limca Gowda, the Chief Minister of Andhra Pradesh attack the unarmed orange sellers who take out a procession to show their objection to the government for having levied unjust tax on them. Limca Gowda uses Emergency as a tool and suppresses the orange sellers. They beat and chase the poor men and women. They let loose lathi charge with iron-tipped lathis. The minister's hired men beat all the innocent people on the pavement. A woman orange seller is mercilessly assaulted and she takes to her heels holding the child in her arms to escape such beatings. Her cart is completely thrashed. A by-stander who candidly watches the scene is severely beaten till he has a head injury. Police have been passive listeners to all those atrocities. In *Manhattan Music,* there is reference to the riot between Muslims and the RSS group in Hyderabad who beat the former with steel-tipped sticks. This results in multiple deaths of Muslims and innocent Hindus. Gautam and his friend Rajan are arrested and put to death by severing the heads in jail. Sandhya's friend Ahmed is brutally murdered with his head hung grazing the surface of water. Children are destined to witness the stabbing of their parents, raping of their sisters and lynching of older brothers. The assassination of former Prime Minister, Rajiv Gandhi with the assassins Shalini-Shalu-Thanu, the plans of LTTE leader Pirabhakaran, Babri Masjid riots in Ayodhya are the instances of communal marginalization. In *Fault Lines—A Memoir,* women community being marginalized on the threshold of marriage is focused. A fisherman and his whole family is murdered for his demand for a fair price and his tongue is cut out by the local gundas. There are realistic portrayal of adult women being burnt to death when their families of origin could not meet the demands of extra dowry in arranged marriages.

Global marginalization is brought to light in all the three novels by the author in terms of immigration. In *Nampally Road,* Mira is the replica of Meena Alexander feeling uncomfortable in England. In her anguish and solitude, Mira identifies her return to India as the only remedy and solution to her anxiety. While the basic amenities in slums are ignored and the poor in slums are badly in need "of a square meal or a tube of ointment where festering wound in a child's brain is infested with maggots", the Chief Minister's colossal investment on cardboard city, arches, cut-outs and stage performances are the global representations of avaricious politicians. *Manhattan Music* has references to immigrants' unsafe plight in the foreign soil. Sandhya and her cousin Sakhi face their situation in turm oil during her walk in the streets and purchase in shops due to her dark hair and brown skin. The board in a museum with anti-Asian images with letters "this land is not your land" is highly disgusting to the immigrants. Draupadi's father Dinkins and her ancestors have been bonded labourers in America. They are called "Paki Stuff" and "savages" being yelled at and pelted at with stones and rotten tomatoes. *Fault Lines—A Memoir* has strewn incidents of marginalization undergone by the author herself while living in Khartoum as an expatriate Indian child. She makes a reference to her friend Solomon's experience of being treated badly as dark skinned jews in Israel. Meena also has had a bitter experience having been yelled at as "black bitch" while she is strolling with her son Adam. Portuguese-Vasco Da Gama and his crew's setting fire to a ship with people on board as a sign to the Indian princes not to oppose them is a staunch example for global marginalization. The concomitant focus on Jalianwala Bagh massacre, the immolation of Syrian Christians, and the World Trade Center disaster during which Meena had wandered amidst the smoke and the smell of the burning bodies in the air lend an immediacy to the novel. She expresses her homelessness of such dislocation as, "my voice, my ignorance that of a perpetual immigrant, a woman with nowhere to lay her head" (Sultana 2001).

"What of this life of rock and stone under the thick green leaves of Kerala when I was living in a desert land so far away? Where was I at any one time? What was I?" (*Fault Lines* 78) marks the core of the theme of marginalization in the novels manifesting with the problematics of existence in an alien land. Having lingered in a colonial background, Meena considers such situation almost like a crossroad of the world as expressed by her in an interview with A. Raja Govindsamy, lecturer in English at Thiagarajar College of Arts and Science, Madurai. Needless to say, Meena Alexander's works have been part of the "great feast of twentieth century literature in English" (Rengachari and Manickam 1995) as she has been rightly called "a daughter and writer of the Indian Diaspora" (Herrero 2007) depicting the real life incidents in a true and authentic manner.

WORKS CITED

Alam, Fakrul. "Meena Alexander" by Nageswara Rao. *South Asian Writers in English*. MI: Thomson Gale, 2006.

Alexander, Meena. *Fault Lines: A Memoir* by Meena Alexander. New York: The Feminist Press, 1993.

Alexander, Meena. *Manhattan Music: A Novel* by Meena Alexander. San Francisco: Mercury House, 1997.

Alexander, Meena. *Nampally Road*. New Delhi: Orient Longman Ltd., 1992.

Desiraju, Keshav. "Wordsworth will Have to Wait". Rev. of *Nampally Road*. *The Book Review*, 16.2, March-April 1992, 25.

Dhawan, R.K. "An Aesthetic of Dislocation": Meena Alexander by Neerja Chand. *Writers of the Indian Diaspora*. New Delhi: Prestige Books, 2001, 141.

Dhawan, R.K. "Meena Alexander's *Fault Lines: A Study*" by D.K. Pabby. *Writers of the Indian Diaspora*. New Delhi: Prestige Books, 2001, 157.

Gupta, Rajesh Kumar. *Critical Studies in Indian Writing in English*. Bareilly: Prakash Book Depot, 2005.

Herrero, M. Dolores. "Meena Alexander's Transgressive Diasporic Female Characters: Healing wounds and fracturing the iconic feminine and the language of the colonizer." *South Asian Review*, 28.2, 2007, 27.

Jain, Jasbir and Avadesh Kumar Singh. "Diasporic Location and Matrilineage: The Poetry of Sujatha Bhatt, Meena Alexander and Chitra Banerjee Divakaruni" by Sudha Rai. *Indian Feminisms*. New Delhi: Creative Books, 2001, 176-89.

Kohja, Sohdev. "Following Gandhi" Rev. of *Nampally Road. The Toronto South Asian Review*,10.1, 1991, 61.

Perry, John Oliver. "Sexual Identity Driving Meena Alexander's Poetic Sublimity." *Kavya Bharati* 7, 1995, 105.

Rengachari, Latha and E. Manickam. "Movement in Time and Place: The Work of Meena Alexander". *Kavya Bharati* 7, 1995, 105.

Sanga, Jaina C. "Meena Alexander 1951" by Lavina Dhingra Shankar. *South Asian Novelists in English: An A-Z Guide*. West Port, CT: Greenwood Press, 2003, pp. 1-5.

Singh, Anita. "Stairway to the Stars: Women Writers in Contemporary Indian English Fiction", *The Atlantic Review*, 10.3, July-Sep. 2009, 115-16.

Sultana, Rebecca. "'Many Souls, Many Voices': Meena Alexander's Reconstruction of Multiple Identities." *The Atlantic Review*, 2.3, July-Sep. 2001, 175.

15

The Cultural Affirmation and Resistance in the Writings of Bama

Shibu Simon

Flag of Resistance

The black and dalit writers explore and expose the exploitation and subjugation suffered by the black and dalit communities respectively to find that all forms of exploitation are identical because they are applied against the only object, human beings. But they want to remind the world that the basic problem is restoration of man to his proper place. They voice their problems or write the atrocities committed upon them to assert their identity and they take a step towards the centre thereby assuming cultural stability. In order to achieve a space for themselves, it is necessary to recreate their past history, which is Euro-anthropocentrically distorted to re-live their lives in the present through the narration of the earlier generation and look forward to a futuristic period of total liberation and equality. Sense of identity and confidence has driven the blacks and dalits to attain empowerment to some extent. Fanon believed that restoration of the past was an important factor in giving colonized people the confidence to envision a future without European rule and a nation capable of future achievement (Innes 10). The writings of the blacks and dalits can be considered to be rewritings of history and there is a metalinguistic critique involved in their writings.

Resistance: A Complex Concept

The term, *muqawamah*,[1] was first applied in a description of Palestinian literature in 1966 by the Palestinian writer and critic Ghassan Kanafani in his study *Literature of Resistance in Occupied Palestine: 1948-1966*. For Kanafani, resistance was for national liberation to accomplish the political and economic liberation of the people from the domain of imperialism. He expected such writings to bring a revolutionary transformation of the existing social structures. In referring to Palestinian literature as 'resistance literature', Kanafani insisted on the need for the revolutionary movement to educate the people to a practice which would transform systems of exploitation whether based on gender, race or class into a collective solidarity for liberation. Hence, such writings were presented as an arena of struggle. The very immediacy and specificity of the historical context reveals the role to be played by resistance literature in Third World literature. The literatures of the blacks and dalits can be grouped under resistance literature because they fight for social and economic emancipation and resist exploitation at all levels. Their writings unravel past history of exploitation and seek to emerge from the depressive marginalized social structure.

The autobiographical form of writing is one of the ways through which blacks and dalits have asserted their right to live, a bid for freedom, and a hope beyond exploitation. It is also the means to express their dissatisfaction in the repressed condition of life and to voice their desires and hopes. Thus, it becomes a literary tradition of self-creation, where women could move beyond alienation through the collective solidarity with other repressed women. Critic Roger writes:

> All autobiography is minority autobiography. Minority autobiography and minority fiction deserve that minority status not because of comparative numbers, but because of the presence of special reality, one provided for the minority by the majority, within which each member of the minority tries to reach an understanding both of himself and the reality into which he has been placed. (168)

Writing itself forms the organizing motif where the experience is contextualized and made an integral part of the writing practice and resistance becomes a strategy in which that writing participates. The texts of such writers emerge as collective corpus, a common statement which embodies challenges to patriarchal structures and race and caste apparatuses. The power of writing maintains the struggles and the writer becomes the scribe for other people who try to survive. The struggle undertaken by Angelou and Bama shows their resistance against the unequal social order and gender discrimination. In that sense, their writings can be placed under the genre of resistance literature which continues to wage a struggle for liberation on many levels and in many arenas.

The act of writing itself was a declaration for Bama. The excessive oppressive force repressed her which generated anger and rebellion within her. She needed an outlet to resist the forces that subjugated her and the outcome was the first autobiographical work *Karukku.* She expresses a desperate urge to break, throw away, and destroy the bonds of unjust social structure. The driving forces that shape her book are the numerous events that occurred in her life which inspired her to write with dedication about her community's need. The politics of dalit writing must be an active one that fights for human rights, social justice and equality. In the afterword of *Karukku,* Bama writes, "It has been a great joy to dalits aiming to live with self respect, proclaiming aloud 'dalit endru sollada, talai nimirndu nillada': say you are a dalit; lift up your head and stand tall" (*K* 105). This short statement explains that subaltern can also speak. She admits the rootlessness in life, social exclusion and the pain involved in it, yet the challenge then is to subject her to the pain so that it creates art. As Hooks has commented, "...the thinking, the writing was an act of reclamation, enabling me to recover wiser to be whole" (30) and creative writing for Bama was to assert and celebrate the humanity of the dalits.

The central concern of dalit writing is with the raising an awareness of the dalit experience and explaining a changing dalit identity. There is a powerful sense of self and the community as dalit which rejects the notion of Varna, refuses to Sanskritize and to evaluate dalit lifestyle according to the mainstream Hindu values. There is a powerful sense of engagement with history of changing notions of identity and belonging. Bama explains what writing is for her, "I experience writing as the breaking of the unbroken and forced silence of the victims and letting the victims and the militants in the victims speak up" (*K* 21). She develops a strategy of resistance that will speak to the muted and create a space from where the subaltern as a female could speak.

The element of resistance in her texts is the strength that she incurred to raise up even from the edge of defeat. She as a nun was happy to teach the children and argue with the other nuns about the discrimination, "I enjoyed standing up to the authorities and teaching with some skill and success" (*K* 20). She was constantly resisting the authorities and was fighting against the injustice of casteism. She wanted the people of her community to be aware of discrimination, resist enslavement and submission and to demonstrate to the world that among human beings there is none who are high or low. She believes, "Those who have found their happiness by exploiting us are not going to let us go easily. It is we who have to place them where they belong and bring about a changed just society where all are equal" (*K* 24).

In spite of all the discrimination and insults, she feels optimistic because she still has a desire to live which boosted her with courage; and also feels proud to believe that she could live in this society which disregards her and her community. In the act of remembering the scenes of insults and oppression, she encodes the modes of resistance that constructs her self in opposition to the hegemonic structure of the caste system. Whenever she questions the dominant upper class authority's hegemonic power, it becomes a political act of resistance.

Bama's works point out how the church distorts the real image and teachings of Christ. The priests and the nuns had frightened the dalit children telling stories of Satan and Evil. After reading the *Bible,* she understood the real meaning of the teachings of Christ, "I learnt that God has always shown the greatest compassion for the oppressed. And Jesus too, associated himself mainly with the poor. Yet nobody had stressed this nor pointed it out" (*K* 89). She found that none had taught her that "God is just, righteous, is angered by injustices, oppose falsehood, never countenances inequality" (89). Jesus was described differently to different castes and the oppressed were taught in an empty and meaningless ways about humility, obedience, patience, gentleness. In the convent, Bama kept quiet about her caste initially, but her anger propelled her to reveal her identity and ultimately took the bold step of leaving the convent which otherwise offered a protected environment. Leaving the convent becomes an act of resistance, thereby breaking the conventions and though she felt unstable, unprotected and unemployed, she achieved a sort of freedom by doing it. She had no regrets when she left the convent because she had a false existence there.

Women in *Sangati* are delineated deliberately so that they gain voice. There is a multiplicity of voices in 'a voice'. She foregrounds her narrative in a heteroglossic structure where instead of a single narrator, many dalit women speak to the reader. She examines the different issues that oppress different women but at the same time has an admiration for those dalit women who could cope with the caste and gender discrimination. Her celebration of women is acknowledged by Holmstrom, the translator of *Sangati*. She admits:

> The ideals Bama admires and applauds in dalit women are not the traditional Tamil feminine ideals of accham (fear), naanam (shyness), madam (simplicity, innocence), payirppu (modesty), but courage, fearlessness, independence and self-esteem. (*S* xix)

Bama explains why woman of lower castes are possessed by evil spirits, why men vent all their anger at home, the reason for the street quarrels, the use of abusive language and submission to the police and uppercaste men. Lack of education and lack of self-awareness makes them submissive and exploitative, "But now, generation by generation we must start thinking for ourselves, taking decisions and daring to act. Don't we sharpen and renew a rusted sickle? Just like that we must sharpen our minds and learn to live with self-respect" (*S* 104).

Her language is lively, genre-breaking, iconoclastic and a constant reminder of the speaker. The local language is formalized and universalized. Her language is completely new and uses the demotic and the colloquial regularly as her medium of narration and even of arguments. It is a dalit style of using language which overturns the decorum and aesthetics of received upper caste, upper-class Tamil. She breaks the rules of written grammar and spelling throughout and demands a new pattern of reading dalit Tamil. She is accused of using obscene and vulgar language in her novels by mainstream writers and critics. But Bama's challenge is to preserve the language of her people and she deliberately uses the dialect of the paraya community which shocks, bewilders and even scandalizes the conservative literary readers and writers. It was a challenge that she did not try to rewrite *Karukku* in chaste literary Tamil but believed that the life experiences of a people can be told only in their language. In *Sangati,* she includes a feministic diction to show how the experiences of women are different from and often contradict those of men. This act of autogenesis, the process of coming into being from silence into sound, is a slow process from marginalized invisibility into central vision.

The dialectical Tamil used by the paraya community becomes a subversion of received Tamil and is marked by certain other characteristics as it reclaims and remains close to oral tradition. The language is purely rustic and without any sophistication so that it may appear to be vulgar and incestuous but the illiterate women are not expected to speak the language of the refined, modest women. The sharp, violent expletives are a weapon to resist the supremacy of the men whether belonging to their own community or to the upper caste. The voice that is raised against the oppressor is a survival technique of the oppressed and Bama writes, "...knowingly or unknowingly, we find ways of coping in the best way we can...we could manage our own lives in our own way" (*S* 68).

Being a Catholic, Bama gives catholic versions to Tamilized Sanskrit words. For example, in Tamil, 'mantiram' which means sacred utterance or more popularly, magic charm or spell, as derived from Sanskrit word mantra, is used by Bama as 'catechism' and 'pusai' becomes 'a catholic mass'. There is often a spin or a twist of meaning, freshness in some of the coinages and different routes and slippages in the way Catholicism has been naturalized into the Tamil of the text. Bama consistently uses the language of popular Catholicism, eschewing very largely the terminology of theologians. Through her writing, Bama intends to break through the barriers that have been erected by an unjust society which has oppressed her and other dalit communities. The ordinary colloquium of the paraya community has reached the mainstream readers in different places, thus, once again, establishing that the dalit community has been projected into public debate or rather to construct their own stream of debate which can engage with and contest the authority of dominant social narratives.

Translation of dalit writing into English and other foreign languages provides spaces for a fair and free global discussion on the subject. It is a development and encouragement when authors could communicate with the world's community, discuss discrimination, resist the hegemonic powers and ultimately establish their identity. Spivak has commented, "Translation is the most intimate act of reading. Unless the translator has earned the right to become the intimate reader she cannot surrender to the test, cannot respond to the special call of the text" (*Spivak Reader* 183). What is demanded of the translator and reader is found in the works of Bama.

Bama's language in her works is at once startling, containing ethnographic details and native idioms. By using self-styled dalit writing, she demands new and different patterns of reading in Tamil. It is powerful because it is real. *Karukku* is the first novel ever written entirely in colloquial narrative style. It is a spontaneous flow which demonstrates how she has discovered her own voice and style. Mainstream critics have begun to acknowledge this sort of writing as radically new and different. It challenged received literary norms in Tamil both in its form and content.

There are several challenges in translating Tamil into English and then the challenge of translating individual styles. The translator's aim must be to make the work reverberate in her/his own tongue. Holmstrom, the translator of Bama, faced difficulties while translating her novels because Bama has depended entirely on the spoken local dalit register in describing the violence towards the dalit women and their resultant deprivation. The major challenge she faced was the inherent untranslatable words which seriously impeded translation possibilities even in middle-class Indian English. Holmstrom writes:

> Even obscenities I find are culture bound. The taint of pollution, particularly attached to a woman can be thrown back at a man. So I have tried to maintain Bama's informality, the rhythm of spoken speech, the cultural edge which colours the strong language of abuse. (Bassnett 43)

The linguistic nuances are of paramount importance and translation can erase the locational differentiations and resistance in their writings. But without the intellectual activity of translation, the works of Bama would not have achieved recognition. Despite the underlying problems, the works of the marginalized acquired a global, cultural perspective and enabled them to transverse the territories of nation to make themselves available. Thus, translation has become an essential life activity for the marginalized writers to move about and convey the personal experiences, emotional conflicts, cultural traits and their challenges and charges.

Strong Survivors

The writings of Angelou and Bama can be enlisted under the genre of resistant literature. They articulate the discrimination and exploitation levelled against their community and themselves as individuals and have created their own philosophy that there is the possibility of rising out of oppression to optimism. They use the philosophy of optimism as a shield to edge forward resisting whatever is detrimental to the gynic quest of self-identity, self-assertion and self-worth. As Slemon has suggested, resistance is found in their texts issuing forth through their narrative style, incidents in life, language they use and it is set against a definable set of power whether it is political, social, or religious. What is embedded in the text is their success in survival, though in the process they suffer displacement geographically or socially and there is an urgent call for revival of tradition and culture. The black culture is brought out by Angelou through the prayers, behavioural patterns taught even as a child, beliefs, customs, and rituals retrieved from memory so that she could valorize and establish that black is beautiful and powerful. The Blues of the Africans are revived by Angelou in her songs and certain compositions and as an artist she identified herself and her community. Bama too writes about her culture, customs and rituals related to marriage or death and celebrates the creativity of the dalit women who compose instant songs to tease and laugh even in the midst of hard work and oppression. All these representational strategies are utilized by both Angelou and Bama, thus making their texts shimmer with positivism.

As Sharpe suggests, the colonial oppressed subject is able to answer the colonizers back. The black community had almost achieved its liberation and there is undoubtedly a progress from margin to the centre. The dalits in India have taken the blacks as models to establish their stance in society and attain social equality, if not economical. The problem of racism/casteism, patriarchy and gender are constantly at work within the writings of these writers but there is a loud call for change in literary and critical perspectives so that the ubiquity of resistance could be recognized, while internalizing their incompleteness, their strengths, their weaknesses, and needs.

The cultural affirmation in the writings of Angelou and Bama can be considered as a necessary phase of resistance, since the culture and the individual are intensely interlinked that it concomitantly acknowledges the need for social change. Oppressed and subjugated blacks and dalits have been silenced for centuries and now they have begun to question and discuss their stance and have began to critically engage in dominant discourse. Intellectual awareness, critical self-reflection and self-analysis are the ways to transform their lives. Those that are 'othered', excluded or discriminated against have to effect their own cures. The optimistic realism in both the writers envisions the future by attaining empowerment only through education because illiteracy and lack of exposure are important factors that oppress them, especially the women of their communities. Angelou's unique style of writing conveys her optimistic expectations and desires for the human race. She is a person who thrives on challenges because she had bailed her way through life relying on no one and nothing but her own strength, intelligence, and courage. Bama's life experience taught her the lesson that life is a struggle and it is when she encounters it with courage and self-confidence that it becomes real life. Her strength is her optimistic vision about life and about her community's upliftment. To achieve equality and freedom from casteism and patriarchy, she equips herself with the tactics of resistance at the social, religious, and gender level. Both the writers have registered their protest in their writings and also contest the neo-colonial structures that try to silence them further. Their literary output celebrates womanhood, liberation and empowerment which transform their works into a potential instrument for the regeneration of positive social values.

NOTE

1. *Muqawamah* in Arabic means resistance.

WORKS CITED

Angelou, Maya. *Singin' and Swingin' and Getting Merry like Christmas.* London: Virago Press, 1985.

——. *The Heart of a Woman.* London: Virago Press, 1986.

——. *All God's Children Need Travelling Shoes.* London: Virago Press, 1987.

——. *I Know Why the Caged Bird Sings.* New York: Bantam Books, 1993.

——. *A Song Flung Up to Heaven.* New York: Random House, 2002.

——. *Gather Together in My Name.* New York: Bantam Books, 2002.

Bama. *Karukku.* Trans. Lakshmi Holmstrom. Chennai: Macmillan, 2000.

——. *Sangati.* Trans. Lakshmi Holmstrom. New Delhi: Oxford University Press, 2005.

——. "The Power of the Word." *The Book Review.* Jun 2007, 1-2.

Bassnett, Susan, and Peter R. Bush. *The Translator as Writer.* New York: Continuum, 2006.

Busia, Abena P.A. "Silencing Sycorax: On African Colonial Discourse and the Unvoiced Female." *Cultural Critique,* 14 (1989): 81-104.

Cudjoe, Selwyn R. *Maya Angelou and the Autobiographical Statement.* New York: Garden City, 1984.

Emechata, Buchi. *The Bride Price.* UK: Alison and Busby, 1976.

Fanon, Frantz. "On National Culture." *The Wretched of the Earth: The Hand Book for the Black Revolution that is Changing the Shape of the World.* New York: Grove, 1968, 206-48.

Gates, Louis Henry, ed. *Reading Black, Reading Feminist.* New York: Penguin Group, 1990.

Gauthaman, Raj. "Oli Vattangal Tevai Illai." *Poi Abattam Unmai.* New Delhi: Vilimbu Trust, 1995, 96.

Gilbert, Sandra and Susan Gubar, ed. *Norton Anthology of Literature by Women: The Tradition in English.* New York: Norton, 1985.

——. "Sexual Linguistics: Gender, Language, Sexuality." *New Literary History,* 16.3 (1985): 515-24.

Glissant, Edoward. *Caribbean Discourse: Selected Essays.* Ed. Michael Dash. Charlotterville: University of Virginia Press, 1989.

Guy, Rosa. *A Measure of Time.* New York: Henry Holt and Company, 1983.

Harlow, Barbara. *Resistance Literature.* New York: Methuen, 1987.

Hooks, Bell. *Talking Back: Thinking Feminist.* New York: Penguin Group, 1990.

Innes, C.L. *The Cambridge Introduction to Post Colonial Literature in English.* New Delhi: Cambridge University Press, 2008.

Kanafani, Ghassan. *Literature of Resistance in Occupied Palestine: 1948-1966.* Institute for Arabic Research: Beirut, 1982.

Kandasamy, Meena. *Interview: The Struggle to Annihilate Caste.* Truthdrive. Com. 2009.

Manohar, Yashwant. *Dalit Sahitya Chintan.* Nagpur: Sangamitra Book House, 1988.

McPherson, Dolly. *Order Out of Chaos: The Autobiographical Works of Maya Angelou.* New York: Peter Lang, 1990.

Mohanty, Chandra Talpade. "Under Western Eyes: Feminist Scholarship and Colonial Discourse." *Boundary,* 2.12 (1984): 196-220.

Mongia, Padmini, ed. *Contemporary Post Colonial Theory.* New Delhi: Oxford University Press, 2000.

Morrison, Toni. *The Bluest Eye.* London: Oxford University Press, 2003.

Morton, Stephen. *Gayatri Chakravorty Spivak.* London: Routledge, 2003.

Parry, Benita. "Problems in Current Theories." *Post Colonial Studies: A Materialist Critique.* New York: Routledge, 2004, 27-58.

Pecheux, Michel. *Language, Semantics and Ideology.* London: Macmillan, 1982.

Roger, Rosenblatt. "Black Autobiography: Life as the Death Weapon." *Autobiography: Essays Theoretical and Critical.* Ed. James Olney. Princeton: Princeton University Press, 1980, 169-80.

Sharpe, Jenny. "Figures of Colonial Resistance." *Modern Fiction Studies* (1989): 137-55.

Sivakami. "Change she Makes." *Out Look.* 1 Dec. 2008, 48-53.

Slemon, Stephen. "Unsetting the Empire: Resistance Theory for the Second World." *Contemporary Post Colonial Theory.* Ed. Padmini Mongia. New Delhi: Oxford University Press, 2002, 102-06.

Spivak, Gayatri Chakravorty. "Problems in Current Theories of Colonial Discourse." *Oxford Literary Review,* 12.1 (1985): 243-61.

——. "Can the Subaltern Speak?" *Marxism and the Interpretation of Culture.* Eds. Cary Nelson and Lawrence Grossberge. London: Macmillan, 1988, 271-313.

——. "A Literary Representation of the Subaltern: A Woman's Text from the Third World." *In Other Worlds: Essays in Cultural Politics.* New York: Methuen, 1987, 241-68.

——. "French Feminism in an International Frame." *In Other Worlds: Essays in Cultural Politics.* New York: Methuen, 1987, 134-53.

——. *In Other Worlds: Essays in Cultural Politics.* New York: Methuen, 1987.

——. *The Spivak Reader: Selected Works of Gayatri Chakravorty Spivak.* Ed. Donna Landry and Gerald Mac Lean. New York: Routledge, 1996.

Sutherland, Efua. *The Marriage of Anansewa.* London: Longman, 1975.

Terdiman, Richard. *Discourse/Counter Discourse: The Theory and Practice of Symbolic Resistance in Nineteenth Century France.* Ithaca: Cornell University Press, 1985.

Wallerstein, I. "The End of the World as we Know it." *Social Sciences for the Twenty First Century.* Menneapolis: Minnesota Press, 1999, 169-80.

Williams, Sherley Anne. *Dessa Rose.* New York: HarperCollins, 1986.

16

Is Marriage a Mirage? An Analysis of Volga's Short Story "Experiment"

V. Sunitha

Introduction

The ritual of marriage which unites a man and a woman holds a significant place in the tradition of Indian culture. The social and cultural heritage of India has set a few standard norms to be adhered to the custom of marriage. This practice is so ingrained in the people's consciousness that any affiliation between the two genders outside nuptials is deemed as illegitimate and thereby denounced and even the concerned are shelved from the society. Volga who writes for women's empowerment has challenged the dogma of marriage and has given a new dimension through the creation of a character named Sunanda in the short story "Experiment". Her conviction on marriage is quite contradictory to the existing norms that have been imposed by the society. According to her, marriage is, of course, a bond that can be formed according to the couple's convenience. Though the very notion sounds atypical and aberrant at the outset, Sunanda corroborates the veracity of her queer thought at the end of the story.

The story begins with Narendra's dithering and dread on matrimony. He has a feel for Sunanda, his colleague, and fancies to have her all through his life. His discussions with her are enriching experiences to him because she can speak on any subject and involve in a meaningful conversation, maybe it is world politics, feminist literature and the pros and cons of existentialism except cooking. But the very thought of her valiant nature and his self-respect inhibits his proposal. He is also apprehensive whether Sunanda could handle ladle and cook. He thinks why he should marry a woman who cannot sate his stomach. He is even flabbergasted by Sunanda's conception of motherhood. Generally, a woman feels consummate and jubilant at the very idea of motherhood. If not for her sake at least for the sake of in-laws and for society, she pines to attain fulfillment as a woman by becoming mother. Suguna, one of Volga's creations is prepared to face any complications and even forego life during pregnancy in order, to become a mother in the short story "Torture". Though she catches a rare disease called Vuvul Edima which is dangerous both to the mother and the child, she is ready to undergo lot of sufferings due to the disease but not to get aborted. But Sunanda has no prospect about children. According to her, having children means onus. She says, "I haven't thought about children so far. When I feel like having children, I will think about it" (17).

Narendra is not as resolute as Sunanda. "Sunanda is firm, courageous and at peace with herself" (8). But he is unstable, vacillating and lacks maturity when compared to Sunanda. He knows that she who has a profound and intensive insight on matters regarding life and its happiness. Her clarity, line of thought, individuality and maturity in handling things would receive a standing ovation. Her straightforward nature evokes trepidation in Narendra. He believes that her thoughts and words are right but she may not be the fit counterpart to him. He is afraid to put up with her astuteness and virtuosity.

When Narendra is in a dilemma whether to marry Sunanda or not, Ramamohan, Narendra's cousin, offers him valuable suggestion. Ram expresses his regrets that his dream to have a wife who could also be his friend remains discontented. Hence his forewarning, "Stupid doubts...only a woman with self-respect will protect your honour...a girl who is slave, would want to make you a slave of something or the other. It's your luck to have come into contact with Sunanda. Why hesitate anymore?" (10-11) bolsters him. Added to this the fact that Sunanda knew to cook puts Narendra at ease. His cousin's advice and his infatuation gives him a fresh vigour. He proposes, "When shall we get married?... Which month? Which date? Even tomorrow is all right with me" (15). Her reply, "What do you intend to do by marrying?... "What if we continue to be like this? This is my house. You can come when you like. When we feel like it, we are spending time together, aren't we? Marriage, married life—being together and fighting everyday like husband and wife—I don't like all this. I am not ready to live like that now" (15-16) dismays him. She feels that living together begets snags to both because, "Each one's way of life is different" (16). She propounds "without disturbing it, can we not love each other?" (16).

Volga's sagacity and shrewdness become obvious through Sunanda. She is sprightly, competent and forthright and she has a clear cut and profound perception towards life. Her sunny disposition would evoke comments both positive and negative. She is an epitome of perfection. Her self-respect and clarity elevates her to a pedestal. Maintaining a smiling face throughout is her specialty. Being emotionally strong, determined and stubborn she proves that she has many wonderful qualities that need to be emulated. Her instinct is to empathize for the atrocities inflicted on women in the society. Being sturdy and robust it is a shame, dishonour to expect privileges for being a woman is her ideology. Neither inferiority complex nor superiority complex overrules her. Her temperament and behaviour may be taken for arrogance and conceit but she is unconcerned about the interpretation of society. She does things according to her thought and word. Domination has no role in her life. She does not like either to be dominated or to dominate. Brightness, wisdom and charm add a sparkle in her appearance.

One should not be awestruck to the fact that Sunanda was leading an isolated life since her fifteenth year. Of course, this is quite common in many foreign countries. A girl's self-respect cannot be deprived by the autocratic man. Sunanda may tone with this statement. In order to live a hassle-free life and to be away from the dictates of her father, she determines to live life individually. Her job and her higher qualification are the fruits of her sweat and hard labour. The concept of family and wife is adorable to a woman of Indian culture. But Sunanda who has already been wretched of family lives alone and, "is not willing to give up that space to rebuild another more or less similar family" (17). Though this sounds stupid or foolish, any broad-minded would applaud and pay a standing ovation to her resistance and guts.

According to Sunanda, the prevailing custom called marriage is a mirage. It is only hypocrisy and folly where she conceives marriage is will-o-the-wisp and a yearning for the outlandish. As an assertive woman, she hardly cares for society and its futile dictums. She detests the ritualistic marriages celebrated with pomp and ostentation and the childish rituals performed by the priests. Rather than living under the same roof like a rat and a cat or like a porcupine and a snake she prefers to live alone. She feels that instead of bothering one's head due to incompatibility, disputes, wrangles and the consequent loss of peace, it would be a precautionary and innocuous to live alone and join according to convenience. She puts forth the same to Narendra when he proposes for marriage.

Narendra is a conventional man to whom Sunanda's words sounded whimsical and eccentric. His hidebound disposition did not accede to Sunanda's way of living because the society and its inhabitants have paramount role in shaping his life. Percolated with the so-called customs of marriage Narendra couldn't come out and have a broad perspective regarding life and marriage. His run of the mill choice refutes to take up unconventional life style. Hence, he prepares to lead a life of his choice. Moreover, he is gutless to live with a girl like Sunanda. He reconciles, "I'll marry an ordinary girl, have children and live happily" (19).

Accordingly, Narendra's parents plan to fix his match with Swarna. Expecting her to be Sunanda, Narendra asks her the details of the New Economic Policy. Terribly shocked by his question, the girl and their parents cancel the proposal. Finally, Narendra's wedding gets fixed with Sandhya, his parents' choice. Things are congenial and affable only for a few days of his marriage. He is taken aback, literally perplexed and unnerved of his wife's grumbles on his mother and sisters within a short period of their married life. All frivolous matters aggravate and take demonic shape in Narendra's household. After many disputes between his mother and wife, he is enforced to oblige Sandhya's crooked plan of living in a separate house.

According to Sandhya, marriage is not a mirage. It is real and a challenging one. Right from her seventeenth year, she has been prepared and trained for her married life. She has been indoctrinated that in-laws are her rivals and have to be severed off. Moreover, nuptial knot is meant to establish authority on husband by making him a puppet and thereby shatter the family ties. Being secured is the predominant need to her selfish mindset and "marriage is her life support" (26). Even in the corner of mind she has no concern to conquer her husband's heart. His feelings are stamped and shelved by her audacity.

To Narendra's mother too, marriage is a defence mechanism, a dominion or power that needs to be buffered. The thought that her authority will be seized makes her aggressive. She indulges in unruly acts. She tears her daughter's half sari and imputes the incrimination on her daughter-in-law. Narendra is paralyzed at his mother's wickedness and her perverted attempts to safeguard her position.

Marriage becomes a crown of thorns and awful affliction snatching away Narendra's peace and harmony and makes him a slave to Sandhya's dictates. Authoritative behaviour, unbridled harsh words, ruthless demeanor and aggressive tendency become the attributes of Sandhya's personality. Her exorbitant avarice and Narendra's self-contentment is a mismatch. Money is her breath, food, and drink. Her utmost hankering for acquisitive wants makes her a callous savage. Worldly things like shares, flat one by one add to her unrelenting greed. In the process of attaining material wealth, her vision blurs. She pesters him to get either his father's money or property. She becomes bestial, barbarous to the extent where she "has an eye on the money that she'll get when Narendra dies" (38). Thus, the couple stands poles apart. They travel in diverse directions in their pursuit to reach different destinations. No one has the least will to defend their marriage. The fissure and the consequent torment deepen his angst. "He forms the impression that she is a devil come only to destroy his life" (34).

Narendra wails, "Does marriage mean one torturing the other?... Is there any meaning to this existence?" (38). Yes, marriage is a torture and distress to him. Hence, "tears stream down his eyes...he goes to the bathroom, cries as much as he can, washes his face and comes out" (38-39) because the society expects a woman to howl and bawl but a male to be unflinching and valiant. He feels mean and disgraceful to cry for the hostility that captivated him. He feels "hell is nowhere else" (36) and it is in married life. While remarking about the custom of marriage, he says, "they jump and make people jump into the fire pit" (29). This evinces that Narendra too conceives marriage as a mirage.

As fate would have its turn, Narendra's aspiration to live a normal life with an ordinary girl gets blown out. His marriage becomes a futile venture and makes him realize the magnitude of Sunanda's words. He is helpless and impotent as things have gone beyond redemption. Lost in the ocean of ordeals and quandaries he erupts his unrestraint emotions with Sunanda. Reveling in the melody of a song, she advocates him to listen to the same. The lines, "Give me those paper boats, those rain showers... give me those nights shortened by grandma's long stories" (31) are blissful but wretched. His anguish and resentment due to the failed marriage cannot dovetail with the ingenuousness and heavenly state expressed in the song. Sunanda holds Narendra responsible for the clash between two women and states that his male ego is satisfied as the two fights over him. Her words only add fuel to the blazing inferno inside him.

The title of the story befits the theme that has been dealt within the story. Life is an experiment and we are all normal human beings who are bound to the insisted rules rather than to its feasibility. If everyone follows the same track and falls in the pit, we also abide by the same and slash bog on us, because falling in the pit and slashing the bog is not a problem as we are perturbed only about the society's intentions neglecting our delectation and contentment in the process. This of course is the affirmative attitude of Sunanda. Experiment is not only restricted to lab and students but to life too. Life itself is an experiment. Shakespeare compares life to different stages in human beings but to Sunanda it is an experiment done in the lab. That's why she affirms, "I may experiment with life, but only scientifically in a very safe atmosphere...in that I have immense peace and happiness. I do not want to enter willingly a laboratory where crores of people have foolishly experimented and failed, where I know if I enter, myself will perish. I'm a very intelligent person. I know the value of my life" (18). She values her life. By sticking to a failed experiment which shows no possibility of liberation she does not wish to pledge her precious life. It is not after the turmoil lessons are learnt. She fathoms it easily by her broad vision. This authenticates Sunanda's broad perspective and forethought. She knows very well that she is not in illusion. Her stamina, steadfastness, calm, cool and relaxed temperament makes her august.

Rahul Narayan Kamble in his article titled, "Challenging the Ideology of Marriage in Volga's Play *The Six of Them*", speaks about six women characters, namely Sasirekha, Rajeswari, Padmavati, Aruna, Sundaramma, and Lalsa. These women characters have come across different men and developed insight into their mentality. Their life experience has made them to question the ritual called marriage. They found marriage to be pointless and futile when there is no love between couples. They affirm, as said by Kamble, "Marriage should give a scope for growth of respectful self, otherwise it becomes an artificial structure of relationship, a shackle." The slogans of the protesting girls in the novel also aver this, "We want not husband and wife relationship but companionship" (489) stands in line with Sunanda's thought on marriage.

Uma in Volga's novel *A Quest for Freedom* joins hands with Sunanda. As a step ahead, she lives with Sudheer. They live together whenever they feel like living so, otherwise they will be in their own places minding their work with no scope to interfere in one other's freedom. Sunanda being a young girl is sophisticated and worldly to anticipate the pros and cons of marriage like Uma. The story brings out many incidents and instances deliberately that reaffirm Sunanda's optimism and clarified perception. She is always sure of what she has to do and proceeds accordingly. Her futuristic vision can unravel or untie any guardian knots. Narendra is unsophisticated when juxtaposed with Sunanda.

He falls in her doorstep seeking consolation. His immaturity becomes deliberate when he requests Sunanda's permission to accompany her when she gets transfer to Ananthapuram. He says, "I want freedom. I can get it in your company" (43). It is her maturity that retorts, "one cannot get one's freedom through other" (43). She bears out to be poised, sensible and down-to-earth by having a sound sleep when Narendra is looking at her the whole night. Her level-headed nature and sense of worth can be spoken in volumes.

Being narrow-minded and nourished by the thoughts of society Narendra has put an imaginary circle. He cannot step out and comprehend Sunanda's broad perspective. He feels her to be perverse and looks down upon her formula for life. It is his pettiness that makes him feel pity for Sunanda. Considering himself great he ponders that Sunanda has lost a wonderful man like him as her life partner. His conceit and male ego become powerless by the twist of events after his marriage with Sandhya. It's not only Narendra but also people who are seeped into the thoughts of the societal norms would rebuke Sunanda's pride and conceit because a woman has to lay her head down and bind to the dictates and be parrot-fashioned.

The letter by Sunanda is the climax of the story. As it is Sunanda's tendency to view things in different dimensions, the letter that she pens has suggested a different perspective to Narendra's problem. She finds fault with Narendra and the society that has trained men like Narendra through the letter. She makes explicit that in the drama of marriage both have equal share and it is not one enjoying the liberty at the cost of curtailing other's freedom and individuality. If Narendra would have got a subservient woman who will remain a marionette in his hands then things won't be so appalling and doleful. She postulates that marriage is an adventurous thing to a cowardly man like Narendra. The strength that a man has is not his earning but bestowed by the society. She verbally attacks his thoughts on marriage, "Just like the eighth class students perform the same experiment that has been performed and proven hundreds of years ago in a very cramped laboratory—you haven't grown beyond that" (47). Through this Sunanda accentuates and enlightens an elevated thought regarding marriage. She aspires a groom to be the one who can bring evolution and revolution in the world.

There is no recipe for life. Marriage is not considered to be a means for an achievement or self-defense or torture. It needs to be lived to the fullest practicing equality with absolute absence of society's interference. Every experiment conducted in the laboratory has an aim, objective, process, scope, and result. It has something to contribute for the betterment of life. The story is an experiment conducted with the view to grasp the meaning of life and the sequel is apparent. According to Sunanda, "One who washes his dirt, his slush with pure thoughts and who in a new and bright light is prepared to experiment with his invaluable life to bring about a possible transformation in the world" (47) is a suitable person fit for marriage.

Gone are the days of the age-old proverb, "Marriages are made in heaven." The story is an attack on the customary creed of marriage. Dr. A.P.J. Abdul Kalam in his autobiography *Wings of Fire* quotes George Bernard Shaw's quotation: "All reasonable men adapt themselves to the world. Only a few unreasonable ones persist in trying to adapt the world to themselves. All progress in the world depends on these unreasonable men and their innovative and often nonconformist actions" (37). A recall to this quotation is apt in this context. Sunanda is one among those unreasonable ones who persist in trying to adapt the world. To her non-conformist and innovative thoughts may add a new dimension assuring a positive change to the existing ideology of marriage. Sunanda's thought may be irrational and may not be feasible. As asserted by Kalam a new dimension may be brought forth to the present trend through her. The writer's mouthpiece is Sunanda and of course her words do ascertain the author's views on men and marriage. Volga says in an interview, "Right from my childhood I wanted a lively relationship with the society round me. I must change. And also must play a role in changing the society around me. I believe that the work I'm doing in women's movement will contribute towards a growth in the society and in me." The author wishes to bring change and revolutionize through Sunanda. She anticipates an amendment in the existing tradition which may contribute for the betterment and growth in the society. Thus, the present article considers marriage to be a mirage and challenges its ideology. Married life that is devoid of love is a futile venture. If love upholds man-woman relationship, there will not be any requisite of the bondage of affiliation under marriage.

WORKS CITED

Kalam, A.P.J. Abdul. "Balancing Defense Technology with Space Research". *Wings of Fire—An Autobiography*. Hyderabad: Universities Press. 2004.

Kamble, Rahul Narayan. "Challenging the Ideology of Marriage in Volga's Play *The Six of Them*". *The Criterion*. 3.2 (2012). www.the-criterion.com

Prasad, Kanaka. *Interview with Volga—Telugu Feminist Poet/Activist*. 28 Dec. 2013. <https://groups.google.com/forum/#!topic/alt.india.progressive/kfntrLsj1DM>

Volga, "Experiment." *The Woman Unbound*. Trans from Telugu by Alladi Uma and M. Sridhar, Hyderabad: Swecha Prachuranalu, 2001.

Volga. *The Six of Them*. Trans. M. Sridhar and Alladi Uma. *Staging Resistance: Plays by Women in Translation*. Ed. Tutun Mukherjee. New Delhi: Oxford University Press, 2005.